Mid-East Wars

the Israeli air force

Mid-East Wars

the Israeli air force

By Lt. Colonel David Eshel
I.D.A. (ret)

Eshel DRAMIT Ltd. ISRAEL

CONTENT:

FOREWORD

From the gallant band of, devil-may-care WWII veteran volunteers who flew for the newly created Jewish state in its greatest hour of need, there emerged a new breed of enthusiastic and dedicated youngsters — their skill and courage forged in the fierce air battles in the skies of the Middle East. From a motley collection of battered WWII surplus aircraft gathered from around the world during the War of Liberation, in 1948, the Israel Air Force has become a finely tuned precision instrument of war, operating the most modern, versatile and effective aircraft and equipment. It has grown to be one of the largest of the free world's air forces — second to none in combat experience.

We have recounted and illustrated much of the IAF story for your reading pleasure. Israel's military security requirements, do not yet allow us to divulge many of the deeds of extraordinary courage and devotion, nor of the many instances of tactical ingenuity and novel uses of equipment. However what we do present in the following pages by text and pictorial makes fascinating reading.

We wish to extend our gratitude to the many friends who have helped us to compile the details of our material, especially Eli Eyal, Lt. Col. (Ret.) of the IAF, and Nahum Gutman, our photopraphic adviser.

FROM RAF TO IAF

Flight Sergeant
RAF: 1942-45

AHARON REMEZ

Commander in Chief
IAF: 1948-51

Flight Lieutenant
RAF: 1942-47

DAN TOLKOWSKI

Commander in Chief
IAF: 1953-58

Sergeant Pilot
RAF: 1942-45

EZER WEIZMAN

Commander in Chief
IAF: 1953-66

THE BIRTH OF THE ISRAELI AIR FORCE

De Havilland Rapides escorting a supply convoy in the Negev during the push south late in 1948. Providing air cover for these vital convoys and flying in supplies to besieged communities were among the chief tasks of these light planes. A twin-engined (the engines are just above the two forward landing gear) light transport and reconnaissance aircraft, the Israelis also used the Rapide as a light bomber. After rigging bomb racks under the fuselage and wings, the plane could deliver sixteen 50-lb bombs in a ground support role.

On a hot September morning in 1914, the citizens of the new town of Tel Aviv gathered expectantly on the beach. A tiny bird appeared on the horizon which, to the jubilation of the onlookers, soon grew into a flying machine that landed gracefully on the Mediterranean shore. It was the first airplane to land in Palestine.

This historic landing of a Turkish Fokker in 1914 was the beginning of one of the most fascinating military aviation stories of our time — the development of the Israel Air Force.

However, the true origin of the IAF can be traced back no earlier than the Second World War. Under neither Turkish nor later British rule did the Jews develop air training to any really significant extent. Although some Palestinian Jews were flying light planes and gliders during the 20s and 30s, the British refused to train them as members of combat air-crews — even during the Second World War. When the war broke out thousands of Jews flocked to local recruiting offices but all the volunteers to the RAF were shuffled to ground crew and support services, and only the most persistent later made it to flight courses. Of the 30 or so who did receive flight training from the RAF or one of the Commonwealth air forces, three later became IAF Commanders — Aharon Remez, Dan Tolkovsky and Ezer Weizman. Remez and Tolkovsky served in RAF fighter squadrons, but Weizman got his wings too late to see combat.

During the war, the Jewish underground in Palestine created a small contingent of flyers who secretly photographed almost the entire country from the air. Concentrating on prospective landing grounds near isolated Jewish settlements, especially in the Negev Desert, this aerial survey was of great use in airlifting troops and supplies during the War of Liberation in 1948.

As the end of the British Mandate loomed ahead, and with it the evacuation of the British troops, the Jewish leadership was forced to prepare to defend the Yishuv (the Jewish population in Palestine) against the threat of invading Arab regular armies. With no suitable aircraft available, the multitude of complex problems inherent in attempting to build an air force from scratch were of utmost concern to the Jewish leaders. They began a frantic worldwide search for combat and transport planes and for trained men to fly them.

While the victorious Allies were scrapping, burning and junking war-surplus arms and munitions by the millions of tons all over the world, the British blockade on arms supplies to Jewish Palestine made the purchase of any sort of aircraft extremely difficult and hazardous. Although American public opinion sided with the Jewish cause, the US Government

Above: *Photographic reconnaissance from a Fairchild F-24R Argus liaison plane belonging to the 3rd Palmach 'The Galil' flight early in 1948. This plane entered the Air Service after being captured from Egyptian hashish smugglers in the northern Negev. Such makeshift World War One-like photographic missions contributed tremendously to the early campaigns both in the north and south.*

Below: *A Curtiss C-46 Commando flying in formation with Douglas C-47 Dakotas. While both were used as makeshift bombers, the C-46s were mainly employed flying the air bridge from Europe bringing in essential arms and supplies, including dismantled fighter planes.*

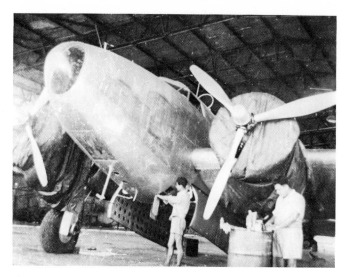

Above: *Maintenance crews reconditioning a Spitfire Mk-IX. The first of these planes entered service with the IAF early in 1948 when an Egyptian Spitfire crash-landed on the beach after being hit by a lucky shot from an alert Bren gunner on a roof in northern Tel Aviv. The fighter was refitted to fly again using parts found in scrap heaps on the abandoned RAF airfields. Another crashed Egyptian Spitfire was also reconditioned by IAF technicians after it was brought down by No. 32 Sqn RAF when the Egyptians attacked the RAF base at Ramat David mistaking it for an IAF base.*

Below: *An Egyptian Spitfire brought down by ground fire at Ashdod, being examined by Israeli technicians.*

Top right: *A Lockheed Hudson twin-engined medium bomber being seviced at Ekron Airbase.*

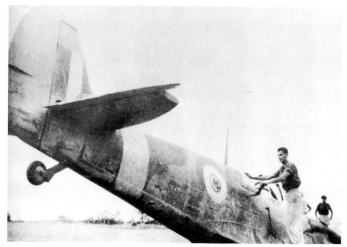

observed a very strict embargo on arms exports to Middle East, and anyone caught smuggling arms out of the country faced being charged with commiting a major federal offence. European countries also observed this rule, mainly as a result of British pressure.

Meanwhile, parked on airfields throughout the United States were thousands of surplus aircraft of all types and sizes, some of which had never actually seen active service. The Government, anxious to help war veterans and also wishing to expand the civilian aircraft industry and services, sold these planes at a small fraction of their original cost to pilots wanting to set up their own charter air companies.

One of these ambitious American veterans willing to try his luck was Al Schwimmer. A placid-mannered flight engineer with great experience in the WWII Transport Command, Schwimmer approached the Hagana purchasing mission in New York with the idea of buying surplus transports and bombers, and flying them out to Israel immediately after its declaration of Independence in 1948. His first acquisitions on behalf of the budding Air Force were three Lockheed Constellation four-engined transports at $5,000 each. He then set about recruiting experienced aircrews and technicians to recondition the planes. (Schwimmer's aircraft renovating operation continued and expanded in Israel, eventually developing into the Israel Aircraft Industries).

The Western Powers' embargo on vital arms supplies for the new country forced the Jewish leaders to look for other sources. Ironically, the saviours of that period were the Eastern Block countries such as Czechoslovakia and Yugoslavia who, with Russian endorsement and against payment in much sought after American dollars, sold arms and services to the hard-pressed Jews (and to the Arabs as well).

In March 1948, the underground purchasing mission in Czechoslovakia bought some surplus Messerschmitt Bf-109s which the Czech factory at Prag-Cakovice had manufactured for the Germans during the war. With the rise of the Communist government, the Czechoslovakian Air Force was equipped with more modern Russian planes and the 'dollar hungry' Czechs welcomed the opportunity of a lucrative deal. Thus, the Jews who had served with the Allied forces and flown British Spitfires against German Messerschmitts, would now be flying Messerschmitts against Spitfires in the hands of their enemies.

But first, these precious aircraft had somehow to reach Israel — and fast. To dismantle, crate and transport them by sea was out of the question — the earliest they could arrive would be three months after packing, much too late to be effective in the forthcoming battles. The only possible solution was to transport the Messerschmitts by air.

The first Bf-109 to leave for Israel in May 1948 was dismantled and transported in a chartered American Skymaster in the airlift code-named 'Operation Balak'. A number of volunteer pilots and Czech technicians accompanied the dismantled planes to reassemble them in Israel and by the end of May a number of fighters were ready for action.

To step up the momentum of the Balak airlift, additional transport aircraft were urgently needed, and the airworthy C-46s bought by Schwimmer were flown to Europe as soon as possible.

From Independence Day, 15 May, 1948, to 29 May When the first Bf-109s were put into service, Israeli airspace was completely controlled by enemy Arab air forces. The north and center of the country were dominated by the Syrians and Iraqis; and from Tel Aviv to the south became the hunting ground for the Egyptians. While the Syrian and Iraqi air forces were still rather backward — flying mainly Harvard fighters — the Royal Egyptian Air Force (REAF) contained all the elements required for a modern force. Founded in the early 30s with the help of the RAF, some of its pilots had seen combat during WWII and were qualified to form the staff, command and training nucleus of its force. On the eve of the invasion of Israel the REAF consisted of two fighter squadrons (about 40 Spitfires) and two transport squadrons (C-46s and C-47s), some of which had been equipped as medium bombers. The El Arish air base became the operational headquarters for the attacks on the Jewish State.

To oppose the attacking Arabs the Israelis could master only three flights of light planes, mainly Auster army liaison aircraft. Though these were useful for transporting supplies and casualties, and generally supporting isolated settlements while the RAF still ruled the skies, they were now at the mercy of the Arab pilots.

The Arabs wasted no time in taking advantage of their position. Early on Independence Day, Egyptian Spitfires attacked the main IAF base at Sde Dov just north of Tel Aviv, damaging the field and three planes. The REAF pilots flew low, over Tel Aviv, bombing and strafing the nearly defenseless city. Their self-confidence proved exaggerated, however, when in an attack later in the day a Spitfire was shot down by antiaircraft fire and the pilot captured. But

*B-17G revving up prior to take-off from an IAF base. The three B-17s were the only **real** bombers in the Israel Air Force during the War of Liberation. They were used to bomb both Cairo and Damascus. Protected by thirteen 0.5 inch machine guns, when in top running order the B-17 could carry about three tons of bombs over short ranges and two tons for longer flights. Two of these bombers remained in service with the IAF until after the Sinai Campaign.*

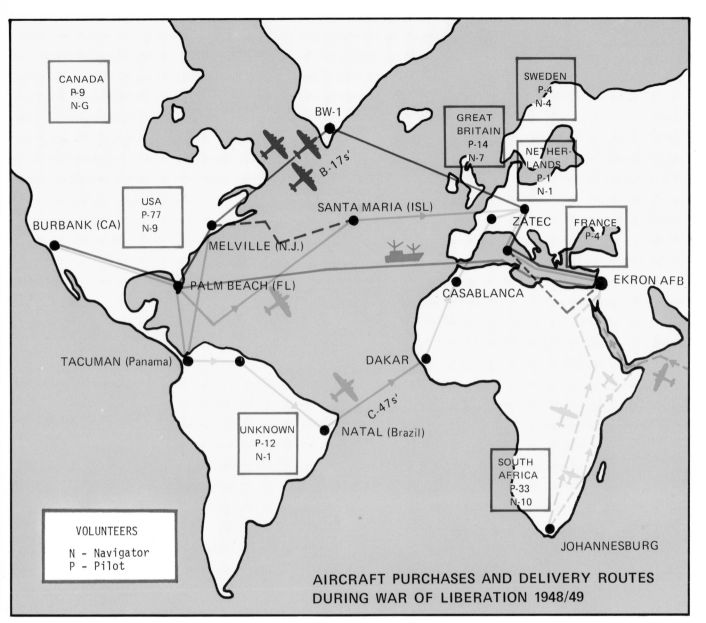

CANADA
P-9
N-G

SWEDEN
P-4
N-4

GREAT
BRITAIN
P-14
N-7

NETHER-
LANDS
P-1
N-1

USA
P-77
N-9

FRANCE
P-4

BURBANK (CA)

BW-1

B-17's

SANTA MARIA (ISL)

ZATEC

EKRON AFB

MELVILLE (N.J.)

PALM BEACH (FL)

CASABLANCA

TACUMAN (Panama)

DAKAR

C-47s'

UNKNOWN
P-12
N-1

NATAL (Brazil)

SOUTH
AFRICA
P-33
N-10

VOLUNTEERS

N - Navigator
P - Pilot

JOHANNESBURG

AIRCRAFT PURCHASES AND DELIVERY ROUTES
DURING WAR OF LIBERATION 1948/49

ISRAEL AIR FORCE ESTABLISHMENT May 14 — 1948		WORLD-WIDE PURCHASING 1948 — 1949 ORIGIN	Number of Planes Purchased	Number of Planes Reaching Israel	TYPES OF PLANES
11	AUSTER LIGHT O.P.-3 (EX-RAF)	ISRAEL	31	31	Auster OP-3
1	NORDWYN NORSEMAN	CZECHOSLOVAKIA	84	78	Messerschmitt Me-109 Spitfire MK IX
1	DE HAVILLAND 89A DRAGON RAPID	USA	73	68	C-46 Commando, B-17, Piper Cub P-51 Mustang, C-47, Harvard, etc.
2	RWD-13				
2	BEECHCRAFT B-35 BONANZA	GERMANY	20	17	Norseman
1	FAIRCHILD F-24R ARGUS	GREAT BRITAIN	16	13	Beaufighter, Mosquito
2	TAYLOR CRAFT-D	SOUTH AFRICA	9	8	Bonanza, Rapide, Anson
		EGYPT*	1	1	Fairchild Argus, captured Egyptian smugglers.
		AUSTRALIA	1	1	—
		FRANCE	4	4	—
		ASSEMBLED FROM SCRAPPED/CRASHED PLANES	12	12	Spitfire, Auster

A B-17G over the Mediterranean. The midsection upper gun turret is missing and the direction finder aerial seen here was not standard in USAAF B-17s. The DF was later discarded and replaced by a gun turret. (The DF was attached by Schwimmer's people to help the pilots on the long hop across the Atlantic [See text and insert opposite page].) These aircraft, stripped of all military equipment, were purchased from surplus US Government stock, reconditioned in the USA, and flown to Zatec, Czechoslovakia by volunteers. At Zatec, Israeli and volunteer technicians mounted makeshift equipment and instruments to bring the aircraft to a resemblance of combat status. On their flight in to Israel, these aircraft ran bombing missions over Cairo and military installations in northern Sinai.

in general, during the first weeks of the war, the Arab pilots roamed freely all over Israel, attacking targets at will, unopposed from the air.

During this time the IAF was also stepping up its activity, though operating mainly at night to avoid the Arab fighters. The lightly armed Israeli planes flew close-support missions in aid of hard-pressed troops and settlers in all parts of the country. For many settlements, especially in the Negev which was cut off from the north by the invading Egyptian army, the planes of the IAF were the sole means of support and supply.

With all restrictions to immigration now removed, the IAF was undergoing important changes with the influx of highly experienced volunteers from abroad. Coming mainly from English speaking countries, these fliers rapidly occupied key positions on the staff and as flying personnel in the force, and soon, English became almost exclusively the operational language of the Air Force. Along with these changes in personnel came dramatic developments in equipment as well as in its fighting capabilities.

By the end of May 1948, the Czech technicians at Ekron airfield had completed the assembly of four Messerschmitts and an attack was planned on the Royal Egyptian Air Force field at El-Arish in north

Sinai, from which the Egyptian attacks on Tel Aviv originated.

As the Israeli planes were preparing to take off on their mission, an urgent call was received for help in stopping the Egyptian armored columns which had advanced to a point along the coastal road only 20 miles south of Tel Aviv.

The four aircraft took off, flown by two Israeli pilots, (one of them Ezer Weizman) and two volunteers. They dived on the surprised Egyptians coming in

A B-17 crew being briefed by their squadron leader.

The B-17s

As Al Schwimmer's operations to recondition the transport planes in the United States progressed, the military situation in Israel deteriorated sharply. An urgent solution to stop enemy bombing of Tel Aviv was of primary importance. Schwimmer had recently acquired four B-17 heavy bombers, as well as some A-20 medium bombers, at surplus dumps in Oklahoma and Florida. Though stripped of their military equipment, they were in relatively good flying condition. Because of the urgency of the situation, it was decided to smuggle the planes out of the United States as fast as possible, without even attempting to receive permission from the authorities. On 12 June 1948 three of the four bombers were ready at Miami International Airport. The fourth was delayed by technical problems. The planes did not attract undue attention among the numerous flights of ex-military aircraft at that time, and the formation took off for Melville, New Jersey — the first leg in the long flight which ran north through Greenland then southeast to Zatec, Czechoslovakia.

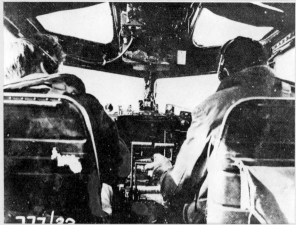
Ready for take-off in the cockpit of a B-17.

The volunteer technicians at Zatec working on the Messerschmitts acquired in Czechoslovakia, set about rearming the arriving bombers with jerry-rigged guns. Ray Kurtz, a former USAAF bomber squadron commander in the ETO, was flown in from Israel to take charge. In July, orders were received to fly the bombers out to Israel, bombing Cairo en route. But the planes were far from ready to fly a combat mission. Of the three planes, only one had a makeshift oxygen system put together from welder's oxygen tanks. This was also the only aircraft to have a bomb sight. Rudimentary bomb releases were installed, together with a motley collection of instruments, making the whole project very precarious and unreliable. But urgency threw caution to the winds, and Kurtz decided to fly the mission despite the difficulties.

After a briefing at the Stalingrad Hotel in Zatec, and last minute instructions for the long flight ahead, the three bombers took off, loaded to maximum with fuel and bombs. Trouble hit them almost as soon as they were airborne. Immediately after take off, he lost one engine and the artificial horizon packed up. Then the air pressure fell, rocking the aircraft in the sky, and as if this was not enough, they ran into bad weather over the Alps losing each other in heavy cloud turbulence. Skirting the Albanian coast, they were fired upon by antiaircraft batteries of the ever-suspicious Albanians. Fighting to bring their rocking planes through the stormy skies, the exhausted pilots finally emerged into clear weather over the Mediter-

ranean, and to their relief located each other again. Reaching the Greek Islands, the formation parted company. Only Kurtz was flying to Cairo, the other two were making bomb runs over Egyptian bases in northern Sinai on their way in.

As he put his aircraft into a steady climb to use the commercial airliner flight paths to Egypt, trouble again struck at Kurtz. As they reached 25,000 feet, the navigator suddenly fell unconscious over his chart table. Other crew members fainted soon after. Beginning to feel queasy himself, Kurtz realized that the pressure and concentration of the welder's oxygen were apparently inadequate. He then brought the ship down to 15,000 feet, until all the crew recovered. In order not to lose precious time, he ordered everyone onto emergency oxygen and then regained altitude. But there was no way of knowing if the supply would last, expended at that rate, through the run over Cairo.

When they reached the African coastline 100 miles west of the Nile Delta, the crew took action stations, some still faint from lack of oxygen. Homing on the RAF Fayid radio beacon in the Canal Zone, they saw Cairo below them, fully lit and unaware of the impending danger. Making his run over the Royal Palace, the bombardier directed the plane on target and released the bombs. Pilot Kurtz felt the sharp lurch as the suddenly lighter bomber gathered speed. Pushing the nose down he set course for Israe, and landed at Ekron airfield in the south at 2245 local time.

Although some 2.5 tons of high explosives had been dropped, mainly around the Abadin Palace, physical damage was not heavy. However, the psychological impact of surprising the Egyptian defenses was immense, and public pressure forced the army to devote much more of its combat resources to defending Cairo.

Above: *North American Harvard, used as a trainer by the IAF until the mid-sixties. This picture was taken during the fly-by celebrating the 29th anniversary of the IAF in 1977.*
Below: *A flight of North American Harvard AF-6s. Though best known for their service as training aircraft for many thousands of Allied pilots in WWII, these aircraft were used extensively during the 1948 Arab-Israeli war as dive-bomber and ground-support planes. They flew many harassing missions on all fronts causing considerable demoralization among the Arab ground troops. These 'dive-bombers' could carry up to eight bombs totaling 400 pounds or eight rockets or two 0.5" machine guns mounted under the wings and one .303" machine gun operated by the 'bombadier' seated behind the pilot. Powered by a P & W 650 h.p. engine, the Harvard could climb to 20,000 feet and had a range of 800 miles. They served as ground-attack planes in the Sinai Campaign, but proved ineffective against the improved Egyptian antiaircraft defenses.*

from the direction of the sea, and bombed the column. Little actual damage was caused, but the resulting confusion succeeded in stopping the advance. During this sortie, one plane, flown by a South African volunteer, was brought down by antiaircraft fire, and another crash-landed at the base. The Israeli Air Force had lost fifty percent of its strength on its first mission. It was soon down to one serviceable plane, after losing yet another near Natanya in an attack on an Iraqi armored column approaching the coast from Tulkarem. When his aircraft was hit by A/A fire, the pilot bailed out over a Jewish settlement on the coast, shouting down frantically in Yiddish to save his life from the angry settlers who took him for an Arab. At that time the Jewish farmers did not even know that they had fighter aircraft!

The Messerschmitts continued to enter service at the rate of one or sometimes two a day. On 3 June, the Israelis won the first of their aerial victories which in time would produce a measure of air superiority never to be seriously threatened.

That evening, two REAF Dakotas began what had by now become routine bombing run over Tel Aviv, when a IAF Messerschmitt flown by Mody Allon suddenly dived on them shooting down one im— mediately, while the other fled. He did not get far, however, and was downed by the same Bf-109. From that time the REAF ceased bombing Tel Aviv almost completely and confined itself to attacks on remote and defenseless settlements.

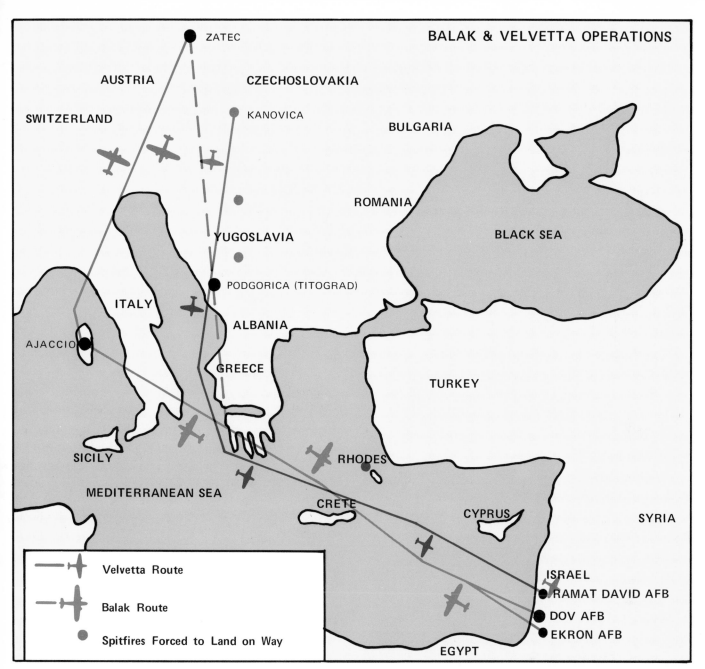

ZATEC

AUSTRIA CZECHOSLOVAKIA

SWITZERLAND

KANOVICA

BULGARIA

ROMANIA

BLACK SEA

YUGOSLAVIA

ITALY

PODGORICA (TITOGRAD)

ALBANIA

AJACCIO

GREECE

TURKEY

SICILY

RHODES

MEDITERRANEAN SEA

CRETE

CYPRUS

SYRIA

ISRAEL

RAMAT DAVID AFB

DOV AFB

EKRON AFB

EGYPT

✈	Velvetta Route	
✈	Balak Route	
●	Spitfires Forced to Land on Way	

From its first secret airlift of small arms until it grew into a shuttle service between Czechoslovakia and Israel, Operation **Balak,** (and its off-shoot-Operation Velvetta), was of vital significance to the struggling new state fighting for its life. Its first flight was a chartered American DC-4 which carried small arms and ammunition. However, the American Embassy in Prague got wind of the trip and forbid the American airmen to continue working for the Israelis. Luckily, the surplus US military transport planes purchased by the Schwimmer organization in the United States arrived at that time to continue the airlift. Stopping only at Ajaccia, Corsica for refuelling, the C-46 Commandos and C-54 Skymasters flew hundreds of tons of desperately needed arms, ammunition and supplies — including 26 dismantled Messerschmitts — to Israel. However, just when the Israelis got hold of some Spitfires, the French, under American and British pressure, restricted the use of Ajaccio to transports and, because no other country would give landing rights to the new Jewish state, an attempt had to be made to fly the Spitfires non-stop to Israel. In

Operation **Velvetta,** the first five Spitfires were stripped of all non-essential equipment, including electrical instruments and direction finders, and fitted with additional internal and external fuel tanks. Flying in formation behind a C-54 transport acting as guide, the flight was uneventful until over the Mediterranean two aircraft were forced to land on Rhodes when the pilots were unable to switch over to auxiliary fuel tanks because of faulty fuel cocks. The pilots were interned and the planes confiscated. Thus only three Spitfires made it. Then, on 15 July the problem of refuelling was solved, at least temporarily. After protracted negotiations, the Yugoslavs permitted the use of an abandoned airfield at Podgorica on the coast as a staging point for both the **Balak** and **Velvetta** operations. The right to this new airfield came just in time, as the French bowed completely to American pressure and closed Ajaccia to the Israelis. However, American pressure was also applied to the Yugoslavs and late in July the Israelis were given 14 days to wrap up all activities. By 12 August 1948 the **Balak** and **Velvetta** operations were closed down.

Above: *A C-210 Avia — actually a Czech-manufactured ex-Luftwaffe Messerschmitt Bf-109 on the Herzlia Airfield. In the spring of 1948 some 25 aircraft of this type were flown dismantled in C-54 Skymasters and C-46 Commandos from Czechoslovakia to Israel.*

Left: *A unique photo of Israeli Messerschmitt piloted by Modi Allon attacking an Egyptian Dakota moments after it, and a second Dakota, had inflicted heavy damage and casualties in a bomb attack on the Tel Aviv central bus station. The first Israeli-Egyptian air battle developed when Allon, a former RAF Spitfire pilot, dropped onto the tail of the unsuspecting Egyptian Dakota as shown in the picture. He immediately hit this bomber which crash-landed south of Tel Aviv. The second bomber broke away fleeing back to its base in El Arish, but Allon quickly overtook it and sent it burning into the sea. Bringing down two of the hated enemy bombers before the eyes of the entire town of Tel Aviv made Allon the country's first air hero. He was killed on a flight not long afterwards.*

The next day three Egyptian ships approaching the Tel Aviv shore with their guns blazing were counter-attacked by an assortment of IAF light planes. While scoring only one bomb hit, the aircraft drove off the Egyptian vessels, suffering the loss of one plane and its crew.

After these victories, in the air and against naval units the IAF rapidly gained confidence and its makeshift bombers attacked Ramallah, Amman and Damascus.

By the onset of the first truce, 10 June 1948, the IAF had become a fully-fledged air force. Though usually engaged in tactical 'fire-fighting' missions

without an overall strategic objective, the IAF had emerged as a factor with which the Arab air forces had to reckon.

The IAF took great advantage of that first month-long truce for an extensive reorganization, ranging from the establishment of an Air Transport Command coordinating airlift capabilities, to sending a group of pilots abroad for advanced training.

Below: *Spitfire Mk-IXE being revved up in its hardstand on an airbase in southern Israel.*

In April 1948, in preparation for the anticipated war with the Arabs, the Israeli purchasing mission in Czechoslovakia purchased twenty-six C-210 'Mezec' (Mule) fighter aircraft. These planes were dismantled and flown in transports to Israel once independence was declared on 15 May 1948. The C-210 was a Czech-built version of the Messerschmitt Bf-109G-14 which was powered by the 1,350 h.p. Jumo 211 F engine in place of the 1,435 h.p. Daimler Benz DB 605 A. This modification necessitated redesigned engine mountings and a broad, paddle bladed airscrew. With these changes the plane was found to have high take-off and landing speeds in relation to the width of the undercarriage so that many pilots complained of faulty landings and several of the aircraft crashed. Modi Allon — Israel's first air ace and fighter squadron leader — was killed landing his Messerschmitt on return from a combat mission.

Above: The first IAF fighter pilots of the first fighter squadron, stationed at Herzlia Airfield discussing tactics prior to take-off on a combat mission. Ezer Weizman, now Israel's Defense Minister, then a young fighter pilot, makes his point.

Right: Three of the first IAF-trained fighter pilots in the spring of 1949. These flyers began flight training on light civilian planes before the establishment of the State. They continued their training during the War of Liberation but received their wings only after the fighting ended. Wearing khaki summer uniforms with the early IAF rank badges on the shoulder — here captain's stripes — light gray with embroidered wings on a gray-blue background. Insignia rank badges were changed after the war, the Air Force adopting the Army system.

Above: *Loading jeeps into a Curtiss C-46 Commando transport during Operation* Dustbowl, *autumn 1948. This airlift brought in some 1500 men and 2500 tons of material to the beleaguered Negev settlements in 417 sorties — preparing the way for the offensive which liberated the whole of southern Israel and entrapped an Egyptian brigade in the Faluga Pocket (including Major Gamal Abdel Nasser).*
Below: *A bomb attack by IAF B-17 on Egyptian positions near Faluga during the 1948/49 war. The hardstands, lower left, indicates this was a former British airbase constructed during World War II.*

When the truce broke down on 8 July, the IAF sent its meagre forces on attacks reaching from Faluga in the Negev to Mishmar Hayarden in the north. On 14 July, the Air Force received a major reinforcement when three B-17 Flying Fortresses landed in Israel after bombing Cairo and military camps in northern Sinai. Now flying 'real' bombers, the IAF carried out numerous strikes, against objectives from Cairo to Damascus. However, the Arab pilots avoided air encounters, and concentrated on hit and run attacks against isolated settlements in Israel.

This pattern of air warfare continued until the end of the war, the IAF steadily becoming more powerful and aggressive and the Arabs restricting themselves to isolated bombing attacks and engaging in only unavoidable dogfights.

The single IAF effort worthy of special note was the airlift of soldiers and munitions to the Negev in preparation for the final offensive against the Egyptian army positioned in the Gaza Strip and El Arish. During two months of intensive flying, Air Transport Command made over 400 flights, delivering 5,000 tons of equipment and carrying more than 10,000 passengers.

Above: 'The Black Spitfire' of Ezer Weizman. The single Spitfire remaining from the original squadron of the War of Liberation, it was kept in flying condition through the years, serving as Weizman's personal plane. Last flown in 1976 in an Air Force fly-by, it has since been grounded for safety reasons.

Below: A pair of Spitfires taking-off from a northern Israeli airbase. The aircraft on the right is already 'tucking-in' his undercarriage. Fifty Spitfire LF. Mk-IXs were obtained from Czechoslovakia in 1948/49, and a further 30 from Italy in 1950/51. An additional five Mk-IXs were rebuilt from crashed/scrapped Royal Air Force or Royal Egyptian Air Force machines. Thirty of the original Spits were reconditioned, refurbished and sold to the Burmese Air Force.

SPITFIRE VS SPITFIRE

Ezer Weizman and his Spitfire — 1948.

Early in 1949 the road to the Suez Canal seemed unobstructed as the Israeli troops advanced swiftly into Sinai, pushing the remnants of the Egyptian army back through their last defenses. However, the British still maintained large forces in the Canal Zone and, acting under the twelve-year-old Anglo-Egyptian Treaty, they delivered an ultimatum demanding immediate Israeli withdrawal from Egyptian territory. (This was in sharp contrast, to say the least, to their apathy towards the Arab invasion of Israel in May 1948 — even though the British still retained military control of the northern area!) Faced with the British ultimatum and numerous political threats, especially from the USA, the Israelis halted their advance near El Arish.

To verify Israeli compliance with the ultimatum, the RAF flew several photo reconnaisance missions close to the Israeli border on the morning of 7 January 1949. Flying undisturbed, they carried out their mission and returned to their base in the Canal Zone. But a more extensive mission was flown later the same day. Six Mk XVIII Spitfires of No. 208 Middle East Tactical Squadron roared low over the desert and entered Israeli airspace over the El Auga—Beersheva road and then turned north to fly in the direction of the Gaza—Rafah area. Mistaking them for Egyptian planes, Israeli ground troops opened fire, but missed. However, one Spitfire was hit over Rafah, perhaps by Egyptian fire, and the pilot bailed out landing near Israeli troops.

Circling overhead watching their comrade descend, the remaining British Spitfires were suddenly pounced upon by Israeli Spitfires. Two RAF aircraft were downed at once. One crashed, its pilot dead at the controls. Another crash-landed in the dunes, its pilot survived and returned to his base with the help of bedouins. The dogfight was short and sharp, as the Israelis quickly broke away with nearly empty fuel tanks.

Although taking an active part in the air war since the beginning, Ezer Weizman, the new Operations Officer of the fighter squadron, had yet to shoot down an enemy plane — a feat many of his pilots had achieved both in World War II, and in the air battles over Israel. From his office at the airfield at Hatzor, Weizman

watched a flight of Spitfires return and land. One of the pilots, a Canadian volunteer, casually sauntered over to him and reported shooting down a Spitfire, adding just as casually and almost as an afterthought — "a *British* Spitfire." Catching his breath for several moments in astonishment, Weizman was amazed at their audacity in striking at the mighty Empire that only a few months earlier had ruled his country. But he agreed wholeheartedly with the pilot's reasoning for his action. To retain air sovereignty, a country must keep out *all* intruding foreign warplanes.

Later in the day, another pilot came in and reported that the British were trying to locate their missing aircraft, and added that he too had brought down a British fighter.

Now that the cease-fire with the Egyptians was about to come into effect, Weizman saw his last chance for a personal victory in the war. Quickly convincing headquarters that a final 'show the flag' patrol over El Arish would be valuable, Weizman took off immidiately, closely followed by three other pilots. Climbing to 7000 feet they reached the border area and saw eight unknown aircraft approaching from the west — which were soon identified as British Spitfires and Tempests crossing into Israeli air space.

Attacking from above, the four Israeli Spits closed quickly onto the tails of the British aircraft. One immediately trailed smoke and crash-landed. The others scattered with the Israelis in hot pursuit. The RAF pilots seemed inexperienced, whereas the Israelis being old hands at the game, picked them off like sitting ducks. Finding himself alone, Weizman pursued a British Spitfire climbing away from the battle and opened fire with his two 20mm guns. The British craft turned over and went down, crash-landing near El Arish. The pilot, uninjured but thoroughly shaken, walked away.

Soon afterwards the cease-fire put an end to hostilities, but Weizman had achieved his goal.

The Israel Air Force continued to enlarge and upgrade its inventory of aircraft after the War of Liberation. The remaining Mk IX Spitfires purchased from the Czechs during the war were delivered early in 1949, totaling some 50 planes in all. A number of additional Spitfires, of the more advanced model HF Mk IX, were obtained from the Italian Air Force, enabling the IAF to phase out the unreliable Messerschmitts.

While looking for suitable aircraft to fill the various needs of an expanding air force, the purchasing mission came across a few hundred Mosquitos on a French Air Force base at Chateaudun where they stood waiting to be sold for scrap. A group of technicians was flown over to prepare them for transfer to Israel. This time the French cooperated and the work progressed smoothly. The reconditioned aircraft were tested by the highly experienced British volunteer John Harvey, a gentile who held the rank of captain in the Israel Air Force. On one of these test flights his Mosquito went down in a spin, killing this brave man and losing the young air force one of its most skillful pilots. Harvey, contributed immensely to the building of the IAF in its first years, flying a collection of motley aircraft to Israel from all over Europe and passing on his vast knowledge and experience to the young Israeli pilots.

The first Commander of the Air Force was an RAF-trained pilot named Aharon Remez who envisaged the growth of the Air Force to a size enabling it to perform missions beyond the perception of his commanders at that time. The Israeli High Command's concept of the future Air Force was that of a medium-sized air corps for use in a supporting role in much the same way as they regarded the Armored Corps. But this was not Remez's view — his ideas went far beyond this. He foresaw the creation of an offensive weapon whose main objective was to achieve air superiority before rendering offensive support to ground troops. Eventually these very objectives became the

basic doctrine of the IAF, but the more pressing problems in the eyes of the High Command were organizational. With this in mind, GHQ appointed non-flying army officers as the next two Air Force commanders. Lack of agreement on the organization and shape of the Air Force and disputes over budget priorities severely complicated the development of the Force during the early fifties. The first Air Force

EXPANSION

Commander, Aharon Remez (1948-50), and the third, Haim Laskov (1951-3), resigned over differences in budgetary concepts.

Though the IAF commanders were anxious to equip their first-line squadrons with jets, 25 ex-Swedish Air Force P-51 Mustangs were purchased as interim replacements for some of the Spitfires. It was therefore around the Mustang and Mosquito, thoroughly proven and highly effective weapons in their time, that the early multi-role fighter-bomber concept was conceived.

In 1954, Dan Tolkovsky, a former RAF pilot, and one of the few Palestinian Jews to achieve officer status, became Commander of the IAF. Under his leadership, the Air Force lost the temporary and makeshift atmosphere that had characterised it from the beginning and became a highly disciplined and professional fighting force. By now the veteran volunteers had gone back to their countries of origin, and young enthusiastic Israelis joined the IAF. The early models of organization were on the lines of proven RAF procedures, but soon a completely new style was devised to suit the conditions prevailing in Israel and the Middle East. The best pilots and commanders were sent abroad for advanced courses, mainly to Britain.

It was under Tolkovsky that the IAF developed the concept of a force relying solely on multi-purpose fighter planes to be operated in two successive stages: first the seizure of air superiority and second, tactical support of land and naval operations. In the Middle East, where most weapons were imported and the wars brief, the effects of 'strategic' bombing were too slow, thus eliminating the usefulness of the heavy bomber.

The IAF started to phase out the last of the veteran Spitfires after it obtained its first jets, Gloster Meteors, from Belgium and Great Britain in 1954.

North American P-51D Mustang.

Thirty of the Spits were sold to Burma, but the Israelis were faced with the problem of delivery. Since the Arabs would refuse overflight and refuelling privileges to any plane which they knew originated in Israel, the Israeli aircraft were painted in Burmese colors and flown to Sicily. From there a British charter company was to fly them to Burma with false flight plans indicating that they came directly from Britain.

TO 56

However, several aircraft crash-landed on the way and the story leaked out. The planes were then refitted with long-range tanks and flown via an alternative route over Turkey, Iran, Pakistan, India and East Pakistan, eventually reaching Burma.

The Israelis were now in the market for more modern and sophisticated jet aircraft. The acquisition of advanced model jet aircraft presented political as well as financial problems which were not easy to solve. After the failure of negotiations for the purchase of Canadian-manufactured F-86 Sabre jets, the Israelis turned to France, whose problems with the Arabs in North Africa were expected to favorably influence the political consideration of the deal. Negotiations were successfully completed for the purchase of sturdy Dassault 'Ouragan' fighter-bombers in 1955. This deal marked the beginning of the era of Franco-Israeli friendship and cooperation which was to last until the Six Day War, and from which both parties profited, militarily and politically.

On the 'other side of the hill' things looked very different. The low-level guerrilla war which had been going on for years, increased in intensity and volume with time. Early in 1955 after a series of Israeli retaliatory attacks on Egyptian army positions in the Gaza Strip and Khan Yunis which caused serious losses in men and prestige, President Nasser resolved to build an armed force capable of overcoming the Israelis in any future conflict. In August 1955, he concluded an arms deal with the Czechs, encouraged by the Soviets, which would completely modernize the Egyptian armed forces. Acquiring large numbers of Mig-15 fighters, the EAF was re-built into a modern all-jet force, stationed on air bases abandoned by the British in their recent evacuation of the Canal Zone.

The massive Egyptian modernization, backed by the Soviet block, presented a potential threat which had to be countered quickly if Israel wished to retain air superiority. As the French Ouragan was somewhat inferior to the Mig-15, the Israelis had to choose between the Dassault Mystere IIC, which could be supplied immediately, or wait for the newly-designed Mystere IVA, which would not be available until early 1956. After intense deliberations and a visit to France by senior IAF officers to watch test flights of the Mystere IVA, the IAF commanders decided to wait, and as time showed, their patience was handsomely rewarded. The Mystere IV proved to be more than a match for any Soviet fighter in the area at the time and it was to stay in service for a long time, flying countless missions with great effectiveness.

The IDF now had its hands full. The threat of the Soviet build up of Egypt's arsenal, increasing terrorist raids into Israel from both Sinai and Jordan, Egyptian artillery shelling Jewish settlements along the Gaza Strip, and Israel's repeated reprisal raids kept the IDF very busy maintaining a semblence of normal civilian life. On 12 April 1956 the first clash between Egyptian and Israeli jets occurred, resulting in an Egyptian Vampire being shot down by Meteors and crashing on Israeli territory. The Sinai War loomed ahead.

The Sinai Campaign which was intended to break the Egyptian blockade of the Tiran Straits leading to Eilat, and to eliminate the terrorist attacks from the Gaza Strip was coordinated with the Anglo-French operation to capture the recently nationalized Suez Canal. At the specific request of Prime Minister Ben-Gurion two French Mystere IV squadrons were brought to Israel to protect civilian targets from possible attack by Egyptian IL-28 jet bombers while the Israeli fighters were engaged in the offensive. As it turned out, the Egyptian Air Force was in no condition to pose a threat to towns in Israel, but the fear of a repeat performance of May 1948, when the Egyptians ruled the skies over Israel, was ever present in the minds of the Jewish leaders and was to remain so even later, notwithstanding the arguments of the IAF commanders.

Dassault Mystère IVA.

SINAI CAMPAIGN

Bombing-up a B-17 prior to a mission. This particular aircraft has been modified and a midsection upper gun turret has been added behind the flight deck — returning to it the look of the original American model. Note the makeshift trolleys for the transportation of the 500-lb bombs. The Israeli Flying Fortresses flew about 200 sorties during the War of Liberation. Escorted by Spitfires and Messerschmitts the bombers were never attacked by the REAF and the pilots would make low-level runs to give the machine gunners a chance to shoot. These aircraft served actively until after the Sinai Campaign.

The Israeli offensive, code named Operation *Kadesh*, began late on the afternoon of 29 October 1956, when 395 paratroopers were dropped from sixteen C-47 Dakotas near the Mitla Pass in western Sinai.

Flying close escort for the transports were 10 Gloster Meteor jets. A few miles to the west and at a higher altitude 12 Mysteres kept the Egyptian air bases on the Suez Canal under observation. But all remained quiet and the only Egyptian reaction to the appearance of the Israeli planes was to disperse their aircraft from their neat lines on the tarmac.

This subtle airborne maneuver, the first of its kind in the Middle East, was the opening gambit of one of the most daring campaigns in modern military history.

That evening, another force from the same Brigade crossed the Israeli-Egyptian border north of Eilat to link up with the Mitla force. Spearheaded by the First Battalion mounting armored personnel carriers, the remaining soldiers and equipment were loaded into conscripted civilian trucks. But some 150 miles of partly fortified desert track lay in its way, and the paratroopers at Mitla had to rely on air support until

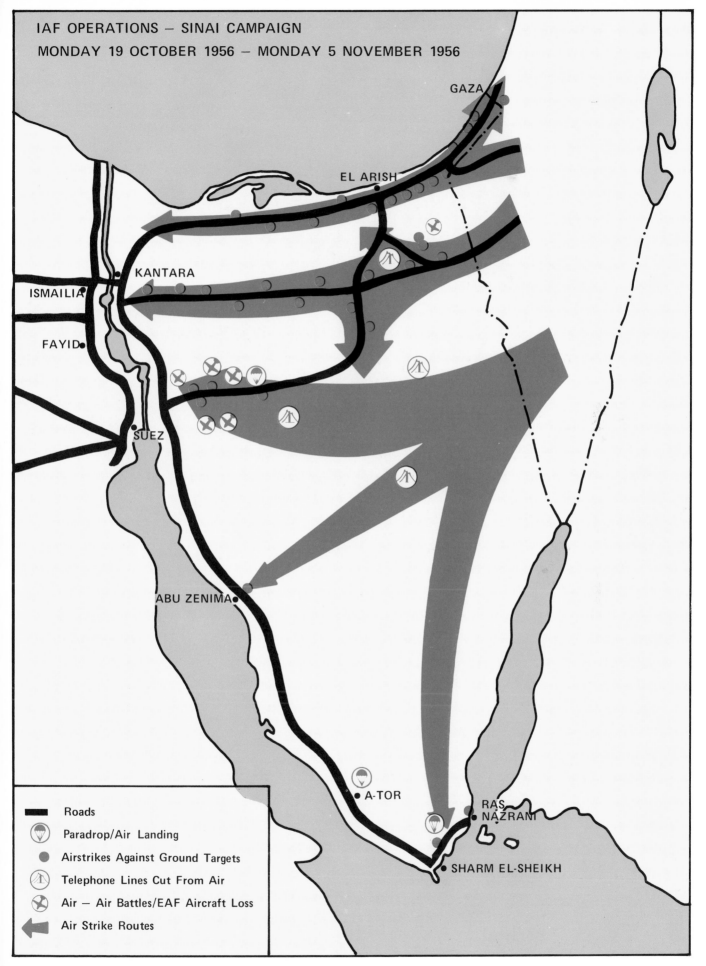

IAF OPERATIONS – SINAI CAMPAIGN
MONDAY 19 OCTOBER 1956 – MONDAY 5 NOVEMBER 1956

GAZA
EL ARISH
KANTARA
ISMAILIA
FAYID
SUEZ
ABU ZENIMA
A-TOR
RAS NAZRANI
SHARM EL-SHEIKH

Roads
Paradrop/Air Landing
Airstrikes Against Ground Targets
Telephone Lines Cut From Air
Air – Air Battles/EAF Aircraft Loss
Air Strike Routes

25

their comrades joined them — quite a risk, with the Egyptian Air Force bases along the Canal only 2.5 minutes flying time away.

The IAF commanders had their own ideas on how best to deal with this danger. However, political considerations ruled out preventive air strikes on the enemy fields prior to the drop. Thus, the IAF was in the very precarious position of having to wait for the Egyptians to make their move before planning its counter-strategy.

Two hours after the drop the transports made another run, parachuting anti-tank weapons, jeeps and supplies; and still the Egyptians did not react. But the next morning, as the reinforcing column of paratroopers in half-tracks and trucks was moving towards the Pass, it was attacked by two EAF Mig-15s, sweeping in low from the west and strafing the column with cannon fire. A few vehicles were set on fire and a number of casualties sustained.

After spending a quiet night deep in enemy territory, at sunrise the Mitla force received another supply drop from French Nord-Atlases flying out of Haifa. The first serious enemy attack on Mitla was made on 30 October at 0745, or some 14 hours after the force set down. A pair of Mig-15s raked the Pass with cannon fire knocking out the Piper Cub liaison plane on the ground. Fortunately, the pilot was not in it at

Above: *Fitting 5'' rockets to P-51D Mustang.*

Below: *Mystere pilots receiving final briefing before mission.*

Below: *A Dassault Mystere IVA jet fighter-bomber. First seen in action with the IAF during the 1956 Sinai Campaign as an interceptor, it remained in service as a ground-support aircraft through to the beginning of the seventies. Note the M4A3E8 Sherman (M50) tank mounting a 75mm gun with a searchlight on the turret.*

De Havilland DH-98 Mk-VI Mosquitos gracefully banking over Israel's coastal plain. Mostly assembled from scrapped parts purchased throughout Europe, these planes entered service with the IAF after the War of Liberation and were used as interceptors, bomber and photo reconnaissance craft until just after the Sinai Campaign. Armed with four machine guns in the nose and four 20mm cannon, the Mosquito was constructed mostly from wood and canvas and a relatively large number were lost through accidents.

the time. A second attack an hour later, this time by Vampires flown from Fayid, did little damage but neither of these attacks was intercepted by the Israeli patrols. The battalion commander called for immediate air cover and the force dug in deeper, waiting for the inevitable counter-attack that it would have to face.

Later, however, air patrols were kept up almost without a break. In a battle which developed in the afternoon over the Kabrit airfield between twelve Egyptian Migs and eight Israeli Mysteres, two Migs were shot down and two more were 'probables'; one of the Mysteres was hit but managed to return to base and land safely.

Though air activity was limited largely to close support and cover for the paratroop forces at the Mitla Pass, there were many attacks against Egyptian ground targets, mostly convoys of vehicles and artillery moving from the Canal Zone into Sinai. The propeller-driven P-51 Mustangs had been breaking up enemy motor columns east of the Suez Canal whenever they could spot them, but the first mission the Mustangs flew in the campaign actually preceeded the paratroop drop by a few hours. They were detailed to cut telephone communications from the Canal eastwards. Flying at near ground level, they tried to cut the wires between the poles by snagging them with tow-hooks designed specially for the purpose. But the device did not work and the resouceful Mustang pilots then dove in low between the telephone poles and sliced the wire with their wings. Mission accomplished.

For the hundreds of sorties flown by the IAF on the first day, the Egyptians flew only forty. The following day the Arabs were more enterprising and dogfights developed all over the Sinai, as the Egyptians finally realized the magnitude of the Israeli operation. By this time, IDF forces had also entered the Sinai along the central axis moving towards Jebel Libni, halfway to the Canal, and the mechanized column of the Airborne Brigade had linked up with the Mitla Pass force, beating off enemy counter-attacks as heavy fighting developed.

Patrolling the sky above the Mitla, two pairs of Israeli Mysteres spotted a flight of Egyptian Vampires strafing the Pass. Diving on the fighter-bombers, the Mysteres shot down three of them in seconds, leaving their burning wreckage scattered over the hills. The Egyptian pilots had been so engrossed in their attack, they had not spotted the oncoming danger.

Unhampered by the intervention of the Egyptian reinforcements which had been successfully stopped by the IAF attacks on the roads to the west, the Israeli advance was picking up momentum. In the northern sector, they now mounted another attack on the Egyptian-held Gaza Strip with the objective of taking El Arish and the northern coastal road to the Canal.

One Israeli light plane pilot on a reconnaisance patrol spotted a glittering object just off the coast of the Bardawil Lagoon west of El Arish. He circled lower and identified it as an apparently intact Mig-15, which had crash-landed in the shallow waters. Navy salvage experts who were called in, raised the aircraft, placed it on a makeshift raft and towed it to an Israeli port. Air Force technicians restored the Mig-15 to flying condition, and it was subjected to thorough flight and technical tests to learn the secrets of the first Russian jet interceptor ever captured.

On 31 October, the Air Force and Navy again combined forces in a successful mission. In the pre-dawn darkness, an Egyptian destroyer, the *Ibrahim-el-Awal*, bombarded Haifa with 220 4-inch high explosive shells. The destroyer was spotted and attacked by the French cruiser *Crescent* patrolling off Haifa, but contact was lost in the dark. Israeli destroyers patrolling further out at sea were ordered to intercept the Egyptian attackers. Shortly after dawn they sighted, identified and opened fire at her from a range of 9000 yards. Answering a request for air support, two Ouragans dived upon the ship and caused heavy damage with salvos of armor-piercing rockets. The Egyptian captain ordered the crew to abandon and scuttle the ship but the seacocks were rusty and could not be turned. The Israelis boarded quickly and towed the destroyer into Haifa port. The vessel, renamed *Haifa*, was later put into the service of the Israeli Navy.

As Operation *Kadesh* moved rapidly to a successful climax, the Anglo-French Operation *Musketeer* to capture the Canal Zone got underway. The general plan, disregarding the Israeli operations in the Sinai, was to capture the Canal Zone beginning with an amphibious landing and parachute drop at Port Said, at the northern end of the Canal. The assembled force which consisted of some five French and British divi-

A Dassault MD-450 Ouragan fighter. The first type of plane supplied by the French, the IAF used it mainly in a ground-support role until after 1967 when it was replaced by the A-4 Skyhawk. Very well liked by pilots for its maneuverability, steadiness as a gun platform, and ability to take punishment from gun fire.

Captain Atkes' Mustang near Sharm el-Sheikh during the 1956 campaign after being hit by antiaircraft fire. He crash-landed on the rocky ground and was taken prisoner by the Egyptians. Brutally treated, he returned to Israel only after many months of solitary confinement. In 1978, as the Captain of an El Al jetliner, he flew Prime Minister Begin to Ismailia — this time warmly welcomed by his former captors.

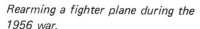

Rearming a fighter plane during the 1956 war.

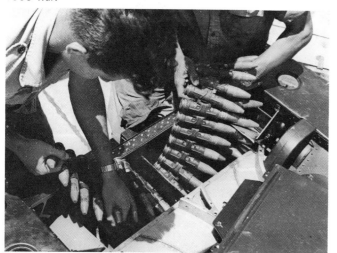

sions, was supported by an armada of warships and over 450 combat aircraft. It turned out to be a classic overestimation of enemy potential.

A massive preparative aerial bombardment was to destroy the Egyptian Air Force on the ground prior to the landing. The EAF by this time was already heavily engaged with the Israelis, and as a result of constant dogfights in which it had lost several aircraft, extremely discouraged. Though the RAF attack on the airfield was not very effective materially, as it took place at night and from high altitude, it was lethal to Egyptian morale. When followed up the next day by a low-level Anglo-French air attack, the Egyptians fearing complete destruction, flew their remaining aircraft to bases in Syria and Saudi Arabia. Their IL-28 bombers were flown to far way Luxor for protection, but they were eventually destroyed by French Thunderstreaks modified for the long-range flight from Lydda, in Israel.

After the unnecessary four-day-long air preparation, the Anglo-French attack finally began by a paradrop and a heliported group flown in from aircraft carriers in the area of the northern end of the Canal. But the whole operation ended in a great fiasco and gave the Egyptians every reason to be jubilant and arrogant even though they had lost Sinai to the Israelis. The vast amount of troops and supporting arms put in by the Allies failed to achieve their objectives due to slow implementation, weak political leadership, and Great Power intervention.

There remained one more objective for the Israelis to attain, in fact the primary objective of the campaign — the opening of the Tiran Straits. Sharm el-Sheikh, guarding the outlet to the Red Sea from the Gulf of Eilat, was a fortified position held by a strong force supported by naval guns. On 2 November, the 9th Infantry Brigade set out from Eilat towards the southern tip of the peninsula, making its way along the coast by a track which had been secretly reconnoitered in 1955. The attack was well supported by air. An Egyptian officer of the Sharm el-Sheikh garrison has been quoted as saying 'I learned about close air support . . . in England, or so I thought until I stood at Sharm el-Sheikh.'

With the capture of Sharm el-Sheikh, the Sinai Campaign was brought to an end. The Israelis had achieved all their objectives in a lightning war of only one hundred hours. The IAF had gone into action facing an air force equipped with more and better aircraft, and under severe strategic limitations which prohibited a pre-emptive strike and raids against bases across the Canal. Four days later, the Air Force had emerged from the Sinai Campaign with a clear-cut victory over its opponent.

A flight of Gloster Meteors over Israel. Some thirty aircraft of various types were purchased from Great Britain and Belgium during the fifties making it the first model jet fighter of the IAF. Of models in service the F-8 a single seater fighter was the majority, other models included the T-7 two seater trainer and some NF-13 night fighter.
The first combat of jet planes in the Middle East took place on August 31, 1955, when five intruding Egyptian D.H. Vampires were shot down over the Negev by IAF meteors.

AIR FORCE WINGS AND CAMPAIGN RIBBONS

AIR FORCE INSIGNIA

1973

1948 1956 1967

PARACHUTIST

PILOT WINGS

NAVIGATOR

FLIGHT SURGEON

FLIGHT MECHANIC

RADIO OPERATOR

LOADMASTER

Modernization to 6-Day War

The air battles during the Sinai Campaign showed clearly that the piston-engined planes could no longer cope with modern combat conditions. The Mustang fighter-bombers had proved to be quite vulnerable to ground fire, and though they had done an outstanding job, they needed to be replaced. The same applied to the Mosquitos and the B-17s, both of which had taken only a limited part in the fighting.

The question was, what aircraft would best suit the needs of the Air Force and, more important, be available to the Israelis. France was still the only country that was willing to sell them modern jets. The French aircraft had proven their worth in the fighting, especially the Oragan which had played a leading part in ground support as it was able to carry heavy combat loads. A new order for 45 of these aircraft was immediately placed.

A jet-powered replacement for the Mosquitos was found in Sud Aviation's Vautour, a rugged twin-engined fighter-bomber which fulfilled the Air Force's requirements for a true multi-purpose aircraft. The Israelis were now better equipped to strike at the enemy's hinterland, countering the Arab capacity to attack Israeli population centers and rear area installations with their IL-28 bomber force.

The IAF was now in the process of becoming an all-jet force. The newly created Israel Aircraft Industries, or Bedek as it was then called, signed a contract with the French Air-Fouga Company, for rights to assemble the Fouga-Magister jet trainer in Israel. The first aircraft left the new plant in June 1960 and started a production line that by 1974 was to produce the modern Kfir fighter-bomber.

By the beginning of the sixties, the Israelis were again seriously worried about the extent of a new Arab arms buildup. Russian weapons were being supplied

A formation of Mirage IIICs still in their original silver paint, over the Jezreel Valley before the Six Day War. The IAF basic combat formation was a flight of four aircraft.

in great quantities and the Egyptian armed forces, especially the Air Force, were receiving, by Middle East standards, ultramodern combat equipment, such as the latest Mig-19 interceptors.

To strengthen Israel's defenses against the increased Arab air warfare capabilities 24 Super Mystere B2 were ordered. This advanced Mystere model was able to reach the speed of sound in level flight, but it was only an interim solution to the problem.

The answer was found in the Dassault Mirage III. Theoretically it possessed a speed of 2.2 mach at 40,000 feet, and with the help of a rocket booster-motor it could climb to 50,000 feet in six minutes flat. At subsonic speeds, it had a combat radius of 750 miles, enabling it to reach far into Egypt or any other Middle Eastern country. Redesigned to Israeli specifications, the extremely powerful and versatile weapons system could also carry a significant load of outside hardware for fighter-bomber missions. The outstanding qualities of this aircraft were evaluated by Israeli experts, and, after the Egyptians received the mach 2+ Mig-21, the initial order for 24 was increased to 72.

In July 1958 General Ezer Weizman was appointed Commander of the Air Force. Trained as a pilot in

S-58 Sikorsky chopper serving as air-sea rescue and ambulance, as well as a general-purpose helicopter — note the red and white Star of David markings on the side. This craft served the IAF during the late fifties until after the War of Attrition 1968/70 when they were replaced by the Bell 205. Twenty-four of these American-built helicopters were purchased from West Germany in 1960. Two earlier model S-55s were also purchased by the IAF. During the Six Day War 863 casualties were evacuated by helicopter. In spite of flying over enemy territory at all hours of day and night, and in spite of a large number of hits by A/A fire, not one helicopter was shot down nor a single mission aborted. S-58s were used extensively in the offensive on the Golan Heights for resupply to the fast moving armored forces and for transporting troops to capture the areas around the towns of Fiq, Boutmiye and Harad, and to capture Mount Hermon.

the RAF during the Second World War, he had served with the first Israeli fighter squadron in the War of Independence and was among the pilots whose attack stopped the Egyptian advance towards Tel Aviv. Having been General Tolkovsky's deputy after commanding two of the Air Forces's combat wings, General Weizman now took charge, and set out to hone the Air Force into the formidable weapon which under his successor Motti Hod would reach its apogee with the lightning destruction of the Arab air forces on 5 June 1967.

The special emphasis in Weizman's doctrine was the creation of a highly-motivated, exceptionally well trained, professional pilot who would overcome the Arab advantage of quantity by higher quality. Constantly stressing this point, he set out to achieve his aim by placing very stringent qualifications on trainee advancement — standards so high that a pilots's course in 1960 ended with only one graduate receiving his wings, the rest being 'washed out'. But his persistence paid off, and the pilots that graduated from the courses were the very essence of Israeli military enterprise, or as they chose to call themselves with no undue pride — 'the best of the best'.

Several air battles took place, especially with the Syrians, prior to the Six Day War. Constantly gaining the upper hand, the Israelis were convinced of their technical as well as their professional superiority. This aerial ascendency was the basic premise for the dynamic planning of the pre-emptive strike concept with which the Israeli High Command prepared for war.

General Motti Hod was appointed Commander of the Air Force in the spring of 1967, replacing General Weizman who was appointed Head of the General Staff Branch. Weizman was the first Air Force officer to be named to this post, second only to the Chief of the General Staff.

The Air Force was now* an impressive fighting force equipped with modern combat equipment. Flying mainly French aircraft, it operated 72 Mirage IIICJ fighter-bombers in three squadrons, one 18-plane strong Super Mystere squadron, and one squadron each of Mystere and Ouragan fighter-bombers. Including the obsolete Vautour light bombers and transport planes, total IAF strength amounted to some 350 aircraft, as opposed to some 800 first-line combat aircraft of the combined enemy air forces, now equipped almost solely with Russian-made planes. The backbone of the Arab fighter force were the Mig-21s, and the bomber force of Tupolev-16 medium jet bombers posed the main challenges to the IAF.

*According to foreign sources.

THE SIX DAY WAR

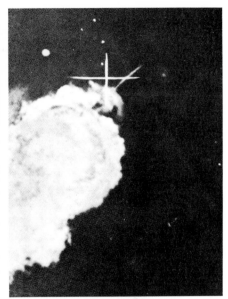

| Tracking | Hit | Destruction |

Above: *Gun camera sequence of downing of Syrian Mig-21 during Six Day War. The Syrians lost eight Mig-21s and three Mig-17s in aerial combat during the war. At the beginning the Syrians had about 40 Mig-21s, 40 Mig-17s and a few bombers. When the Syrians, Jordanians and Iraqis attacked targets in Israel during the morning of 5 June the IAF had already finished off the Egyptian Air Force and could quickly deal with these. Within one hour two-thirds of the Syrian Air Force was destroyed.*

Below: *Samoa, Jordan 1967. A Royal Jordanian Air Force Hunter Mk-IX shot down by IAF jets in a dogfight during an Israeli retaliatory raid prior to the Six Day War. The rocky heights on the left are the hills of Judea near the Dead Sea. The Jordanian pilots showed a high standard of training and fighting spirit in these air battles.*

| Tracking | Destruction |

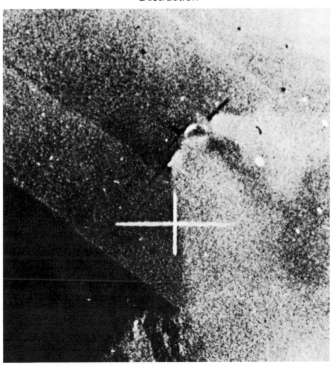

At 0745 on Monday, 5 June 1967 the Israeli Air Force struck simultaneously at ten Egyptian airfields. Two pairs of aircraft concentrated on each target field, strafing parked planes, bombing runways and destroying antiaircraft defenses. Three of the airfields attacked were in Sinai — El Arish, Jebel Libni and Bir Gafgafa — the others were major airfields in the Canal Zone and the Delta. The Egyptian Air Force was caught on the ground, while its pilots were quietly enjoying their breakfast, having flown their usual dawn patrol some time earlier.

A single Egyptian plane was airborne: a twin-engined Illyushin heading westward over Sinai and carrying three of the highest ranking Egyptian commanders including the Chief of Staff, General Amer. Listening in on the Israeli frequencies, the commanders could not make out any unusual traffic, and flying west the Illyushin headed for Kabrit airbase. At that precise moment the control tower informed the pilot that it was under air attack. Confused by chatter which covered all frequencies with excited announcements that all airbases were being attacked, the commanders, in complete frustration, vainly tried to find a base where they could land. As they searched they watched the bases along the whole length of the Canal going up in flames. They finally landed at Cairo International Airport and rushed to the Command Room — only to be informed that for all practical purposes the Egyptian Air Force no longer existed.

For two hours the IAF ravaged the Egyptian airfields; as each flight of four fighter-bombers completed its attack   the next formation of four took over. The

Above: *A last minute check before take-off at dawn.*

Below: *0630 hours 5 June 1967 at an IAF airbase. The fuel tanker is filling up the Mirage IIIC on which the ground crew has worked all night readying the aircraft for this mission. Matra R-530 air-to-air missile and drop tanks indicate this plane is assigned an interceptor, high cover, or air superiority role.*

Above: A Dassault Super Mystere B-2 jet fighter-bomber pilot strapped into his seat. The hood is already closed for take-off — target Egypt. Along the top canopy brace can be seen two rear-view mirrors. The transparent rectangle below the left mirror is the gun sight. For an interesting comparison note the difference between the pilot's instrumentation in the Super Mystere and that of the two-generations more modern F-15 Eagle on page 74.

Below: Mirage IIIC unsticking from the runway en route for a combat patrol. Fuel drop tanks under both wings enable long distance standing patrols as top cover for attacking fighter-bombers. IAF Mirage interceptors often flew without missiles, depending only on their 30mm cannons, to permit extended air time.

results of the precise air strikes far surpassed the expectations of the Israeli commanders and stunned the world.

At Cairo West airfield, the Israeli Mirages caught all 30 of the Egyptian Tu-16 bombers parked in their hard-stands and blew them to pieces, eliminating the danger to the Israeli cities posed by the EAF. Twin-engined Vautours crossed the Red Sea and streaked deep into Upper Egypt to destroy the planes at Luxor and Ras Banas, where the Egyptians had dispersed their aircraft in search of safety.

Above left: A Mig-21 destroyed on the runway — the pilot hastily abandoned the aircraft before it went up in flames.
Above right: Morning, 6 June 1967 — Cairo West airfield under IAF attack. Note the neatly lined up transports on the far side of the runway. Many were destroyed in the first surprise attack. Within sight of Cairo, this was one of the most important Egyptian airfields and was protected by five SAM-2 batteries and dozens of A/A machine guns and cannons. During the morning of 5 June all ten of the main Egyptian military airfields were attacked: first putting the runways out of service and then destroying most of the planes stationed at each base. Over 300 aircraft were smashed within only three hours.

Below: Entrance to Mitla Pass, June 1967. Egyptian military convoys destroyed by IAF fighter-bombers.

H-HOUR

There were four reasons why the Israelis chose 0745 (Israel time) as the hour for attack:

1. The Egyptian state of alert was past its peak. It was safe to assume that the Egyptians, ever since they began their concentration of troops in Sinai three weeks earlier, had several flights of Mig-21s waiting at the end of the runway on 5-minute alert at dawn every morning. They were also probably flying one or two Mig-21 airborne patrols at this time of day, a most likely time for an an enemy to attack.

However, it was calculated to be most unlikely that they would have stayed at this state of readiness indefinitely. When no attack had materialized within two or three hours after dawn the Egyptians would more than likely have lessened their alert and switched off their radar scanners. The Israelis felt it safe to assume that by 0730 (0830 Cairo time) the Egyptians had lowered their guard.

2. Very often attacks are made at dawn. But since pilots have to be on deck at least three hours before getting airborne, that would have meant their getting up at about midnight or in fact getting no sleep at all that night. By the evening of the first day of war they would have had no sleep for 36 hours with the possibility of a further night and a whole day of combat missions ahead of them. By making the initial strike at 0745 the pilots were able to sleep until 0400.

3. At this time of the year there is a morning mist over much of the Nile, the Delta and the Suez Canal. By 0730 this mist had just about dispersed. Around 0800 the weather is usually at its optimum. The visibility is at its best because of the angle of the sun, and the air is at its stillest, which is important when it comes to placing bombs accurately on runways.

4. 0745 Israel time is 0845 Egypt time. Why 0745 rather than 0800 or 0815? It's because Egyptians get to their offices at 9 a.m. Striking 15 minutes before that time would catch generals and air force commanders on their way to their offices, and pilots and air force personnel on their way to training courses and other activities.

General Hod was in the command center when the last of the Egyptian early morning patrols got airborne and appeared on the Israeli radar screens. He pressed his stopwatch. He knew very well how long the Mig-21 can stay airborne — by 0745 the

patrol would be almost out of fuel and on the point of landing.

The primary objectives of the first strike were to make the runways unusable and destroy as many Mig-21s as possible. The Mig-21s were the only Egyptian aircraft that could effectively prevent the Israeli air force from achieving its objective — the destruction of Egypt's long-range bomber force which posed such a threat to the civilian population of Israel.

Eight formations of Mig-21s were destroyed as they were taxiing to the end of the runways. Earlier the Israelis had managed to induce the Egyptians to move 20 of their frontline aircraft — 12 Mig-21s and 8 Mig-19's — from the area around Cairo and the Canal where Egypt's major air bases were concentrated, to Hurghada in the south where they were effectively hors de combat. The Israelis had achieved this a few days earlier by sending several test flights to the south over the Gulf of Aqaba which persuaded the Egyptians that the Israelis might well be planning to attack with a left hook around the southern end of the Sinai Peninsula instead of, as in fact was the case, by a right hook out over the Mediterranean.

These twenty Migs, once the Israeli sledge hammer had fallen, instead of heading south to Luxor and other bases in Upper Egypt, to which they might have been able to afford at least some protection, headed north to the bases near the Canal where they found they had no runways to land on. They fell prey to the Israeli Air Force.

Mirage fighter pilots in G-suits carrying dome type helmets. during the six days, IAF pilots destroyed over 450 Arab combat planes on the ground or in the air, opening the way for the ground troops to complete the victory. By the end of the war, the attack sorties were divided one-third to gain air superiority and two-thirds in support of ground troops.

Though most of the Arab planes were destroyed on the ground, some dogfights nevertheless developed. The largest one took place over Abu Suweir near Ismailia, where 16 Mirages and 20 Mig-21s clashed high over the battle zone. The Egyptians courageously hurled themsleves at the Israelis, but four of them were shot down within a few seconds and the remainder scattered, trying to land on the bomb-pitted runways of their airfields, many crashing in the attempt. Influenced by Egyptian boasts of their ascendancy

over the Jewish State, Jordanian and Iraqi aircraft attacked targets in Israel. Having already crushed the Egyptian Air Force, the IAF struck back at the Jordanian, Syrian and Iraqi airforces, putting them out of commission by midday.

The ground war could now pursue its objectives, supported by a victorious air force that could operate at will over the battlefield. Battles were raging on all three borders. In the west, the Israeli armored divisions

Israeli jet fighter pilots returning from a combat mission. The officer on the left — a lieutenant — is wearing G-suit trousers, a light khaki shirt over which he is wearing an inflatable life jacket. The boxes contain gun camera film.

advanced into Sinai with the objective of reaching the Suez Canal.

On the second day of the fighting, Algerian Mig-21s which had been rushed to the battle area, made several surprise attacks, mainly on the coastal sector in the north of Sinai. Though effective, they could not replace the strength of the shattered Egyptian force.

On the eastern front, the Israeli attack on the West Bank gained momentum with the capture of Jerusalem and the hills of Samaria, thus bringing to an end Jordanian rule over the territories annexed in 1948. In the heavy fighting for the Old City of Jerusalem, the Israeli fighter-bombers strafed Jordanian army positions on Mount Scopus enabling the Israeli paratroopers to capture their objectives.

The most intense bombing and strafing of the war was directed against the Syrian fortified Golan Heights.

Sud Aviation SA-4050 Vautour single-seat light bomber landing on a northern IAF airbase. The braking chute is out helping stop the airplane. Later versions were painted with camouflage colors. These aircraft flew long-range bombing missions as far between as the upper Nile Valley in Egypt and Iraqi airfields during the Six Day War.

This major obstacle was subjected to heavy bombing, which was ineffective because the well dug-in fortification were almost impenetrable. This necessitated hand-to-hand fighting, with the Air Force holding off enemy reinforcements and attacking concentrations of artillery inside Syrian territory. It was during this fighting that the Russian SAM-2 surface-to-air missile was first encountered. Though they did not succeed in downing an Israeli plane, they were to have an immense impact on the combat environment in future ones.

When the cease-fire came into force on Saturday, 10 June, the IAF had lost a total of 46 aircraft, all but three of which were brought down by ground fire. Some badly damaged planes had crashed on return to their base and a few pilots had bailed out over enemy territory and were taken prisoner. For an air force that started the war with less than 200* combat aircraft, this was a serious loss. However, the crushing blow that had been dealt to the enemy in destroying some 450 of their aircraft in so short a time gave the elated aircrews an overwhelming sense of victory. On the other hand, they were under no illusions that the fighting was over and the final battle won.

*According to foreign sources.

Above: *Super Mystere B-2 in power take-off. The first true supersonic aircraft in the IAF, it served as the front-line fighter from 1958 until the arrival of the Mirage in 1963.*

Below Right: *Ground-support mission of a Mystere IVA on the hills of East Jerusalem during the Six Day War.*

Above: *Ground-support bombing of Egyptian positions at last light in Sinai.*

Facing: *A Sud Aviation Potez-Air Fouga CM 170 Magister jet trainer during the 1967 war. These aircraft were armed with 0.3" machine guns, 12 to 16 80mm rockets or four 100-lb bombs and flown by reserve pilots, carried out ground-attack missions during the Six Day War on the Egyptian and Jordanian fronts. Already on the first day the Fougas destroyed three radar stations, 40 tanks, an ammunition train, and many light vehicles. Lacking an ejection seat and too slow to evade A/A fire or enemy fighters, the Fougas were dangerous aircraft to fly. Note stencils on fuselage — this plane has already taken out two trucks and a tank.*

Above: *North American Harvard AT-6 trainers at Sirkin Flying School near Tel Aviv lined up for inspection.*

Left: *A line of light observation Piper Cubs — army liaison aircraft used for directing artillery fire, flying out casualties and in many daring missions far into the enemy's rear areas.*

Bottom left: *The student needed a few more lessons on his Boeing Stearman. This American-built bi-plane was used as a trainer during the fifties.*

Pilot Training

The IAF pilot training program lasts for 20 months, divided into five stages:

1. Potential pilots are first taught to fly light aircraft. This is considered more of a practical selection test rather than an actual teaching course.

2. The trainee pilots are then given courses in mathematics, physics, meteorology, aeronautics, electronics, navigation and weaponry. This intensive, though in many aspects rather superficial, applied science education provides aircrews with an understanding of the inner workings of the equipment they operate, as opposed to other air forces' 'black box' attitudes towards instrumentation where the aircrew learns only functional operation.

3. Next comes a stage of intensive physical training and endurance trials. The trainees are also taught general and acrobatic flying with jet trainers. Demands are severe and a large percentage of trainees drop out at this stage.

4. Training concentrates at this stage on day and night flying, and at this point the final selection of potential combat pilots is made.

5. Now the trainee receives an intensive series of flight period of air-to-air and air-to-ground exercises to prepare him for operational duty.

Overleaf: *Cadets carry unit flags in review on Air Force Day.*

THE TRAINING SCHOOL

The Aerobatic Team

Above: *A Noratlas 2501 low over the Sinai Desert moving supplies. Note the rear door has been removed in order to parachute supplies and equipment to ground forces.*
Below: *A Sud Aviation SA-321 Superfrelon helicopter, then the heaviest and most up-to-date helicopter in the IAF, setting down near a group of Israeli reconnaissance vehicles in Sinai. These aircraft saved many lives by carrying supplies to combat areas and returning with casualties to rear hospitals.*

A girl flight controller operating her portable radio on a temporary transport airfield somewhere in Sinai.

A 'standby' S-58 helicopter being alerted for a rescue mission.

WAR OF ATTRITION

Against the guerrillas. *A Bell 205 giving support to an anti-guerrilla search in the Hebron hills. Operating in a tightly integrated force with crack paratroopers, the helicopter pilots flew countless missions helping to break the back of the PLO guerrilla activities which made life difficult on the frontiers.*

Immediately after the cease-fire of June 1967 the Russians again rebuilt the shattered Arab forces. A vast Soviet airlift replenished the Arab arsenals so quickly that by the end of June 1967, only two weeks after the defeat, the Egyptians had almost 200 aircraft, mainly Mig-21s and Sukhoi-7s — an air force more modern and formidable than the one annihilated by the Israelis. The Arabs, who had learned their lesson from the air strike that destroyed their air forces on the ground, now widely dispersed their planes in underground hangars with thick concrete roofs. Since most of the aircraft had been destroyed on the ground, the Egyptians had lost only a few air crews in the fighting and thus were at no loss for trained personnel to man the new planes. Furthermore, the Soviets agreed to train hundreds of pilots in their flying schools in Russia.

Israel, however, found it difficult to acquire replacement aircraft. The loss of some 40 planes in the war, with a few additional damaged, seriously diminished

the IAF's inventory. The one-sided French embargo imposed before the war was holding up delivery of 50 custom designed and paid for Mirage Vs. The Americans also became evasive about fulfilling their commitment to supply Skyhawks, which they finally honored towards the latter part of the year.

The Egyptians, gaining confidence with the growing stream of arms and not wanting the status quo to solidify, began intermittently shelling Israeli positions along the Suez Canal. The Israelis, unable to match the massive Egyptian artillery force, dug in and prepared to absorb the blows, hitting back here and there with deep penetration commando raids. Early in 1969, the Egyptians intensified the conflict by suddenly opening up with an extremely heavy artillery bombardment, causing heavy casualties among the Israeli troops. In the subsequent 48 hours more than *35,000* shells fell on the Israelis who retaliated by setting fire to the Egyptian oil refineries in Suez City.

Against the Egyptians. *McDonnel Douglas A-4 Skyhawk fighter-bomber — the workhorse of the IAF — over the Sinai hills. These were the first American-manufactured combat aircraft officially supplied to the IAF. (Earlier many American planes were bought as surplus and scrap.)*

The Egyptian bombardments continued. Risking confrontation with the new missile defense system and the possibility of escalation into another full scale war, the Israelis introduced their 'flying artillery', the Air Force, into the fighting.

On 29 July 1969, the IAF struck at the Egyptians: first hitting the missile sites, antiaircraft gun batteries and radar installations, then bombing the artillery positions. The stunned Egyptians hardly reacted to this onslaught, and the Egyptian Air Force stayed out of the fight. Only three hours later, while the Israeli pilots were still harassing the Egyptian positions, did the EAF finally show its hand. A flight of Sukhoi-7s and Mig-17s struck in a low-level hit and run attack into Sinai causing little damage. However, the Israeli high cover interceptors fell on the attackers and shot down five Egyptian aircraft for one Israeli plane hit.

Working systematically at destroying the Egyptian positions during the subsequent weeks, the IAF

encountered almost no Egyptian aircraft. That the Egyptian reticence was well advised, was evidenced when in an encounter with the IAF two months later, the EAF lost 11 planes in dogfights. This was the largest 'bag' of jets downed in one aerial combat in history, one Israeli pilot bringing his personal score up to eight jets. The Egyptian army's morale now began to founder seriously, as the IAF again proved its ability to dominate the skies.

While the fighting was going on along and over the Canal, the Air Force also had its role to play in the fight against the guerillas and their Arab regular army backing on the Jordanian Front. By this time the Iraqis had also entered Jordan with a strong force concentrated around Irbid in the north opposite the Israeli side of the Jordan River Valley.

The PLO guerillas were not making much headway in their efforts to infiltrate into Israel and to support them the Iraqis and Jordanians began shelling Jewish

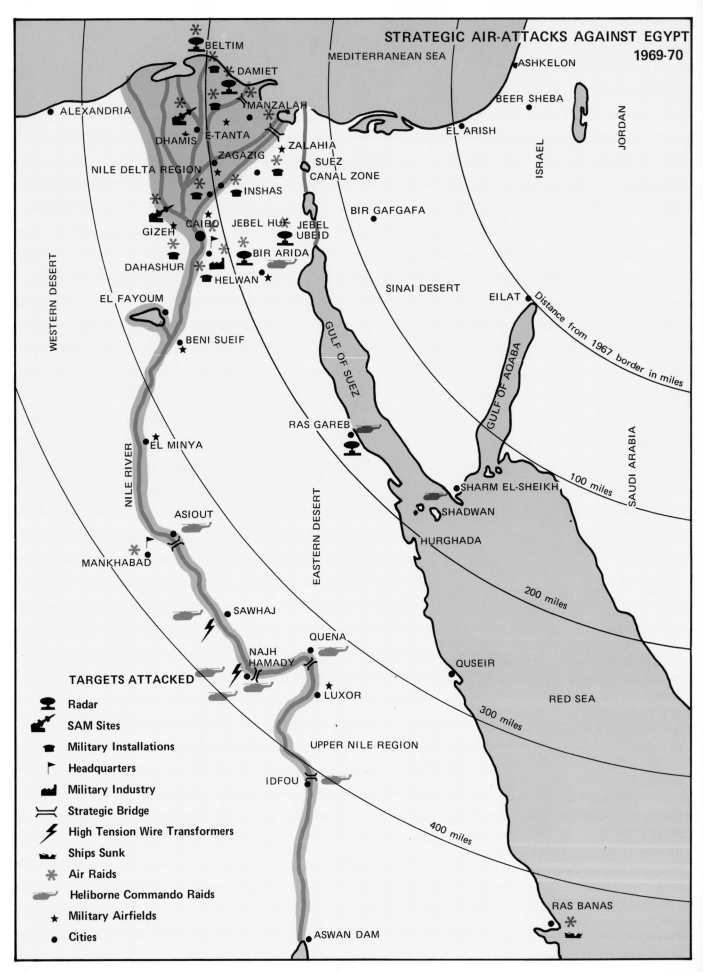

STRATEGIC AIR-ATTACKS AGAINST EGYPT
1969-70

MEDITERRANEAN SEA

ASHKELON

BEER SHEBA

BELTIM

DAMIET

ALEXANDRIA

MANZALAH

EL ARISH

DHAMIS

E-TANTA

ISRAEL

JORDAN

ZALAHIA

ZAGAZIG

SUEZ

NILE DELTA REGION

CANAL ZONE

INSHAS

BIR GAFGAFA

GIZEH

CAIRO

JEBEL HUF

JEBEL UBEID

DAHASHUR

BIR ARIDA

HELWAN

SINAI DESERT

EILAT

EL FAYOUM

WESTERN DESERT

BENI SUEIF

GULF OF SUEZ

GULF OF AQABA

Distance from 1967 border in miles

SAUDI ARABIA

NILE RIVER

EL MINYA

RAS GAREB

100 miles

SHARM EL-SHEIKH

ASIOUT

SHADWAN

MANKHABAD

HURGHADA

EASTERN DESERT

200 miles

SAWHAJ

QUENA

QUSEIR

NAJH HAMADY

RED SEA

300 miles

LUXOR

TARGETS ATTACKED

UPPER NILE REGION

IDFOU

400 miles

	Radar
	SAM Sites
	Military Installations
	Headquarters
	Military Industry
	Strategic Bridge
	High Tension Wire Transformers
	Ships Sunk
	Air Raids
	Heliborne Commando Raids
	Military Airfields
	Cities

RAS BANAS

ASWAN DAM

Sikorsky CH-53 heavy transport helicopter. Able to lift 4.5 tons with a full fuel load over a range of 280 miles, these aircraft are the main transporters for heliborne combat troops.

settlements in the valley. The Air Force was again called in to stop the artillery harassment. On 12 December the IAF subjected the Iraqis to a smashing blow, bombing their installations and artillery concentrations and causing heavy losses to men and material.

Then the Syrians joined in the fight. Shelling started all along the Golan Heights and the Israelis retaliated by bombing El Fatah camps near Damascus. In one dogfight between Syrian and Israeli planes over Damascus, a Mig-17 was shot down by a Skyhawk still carrying its full load — an unprecedented feat. It became clear that the Israeli pilots still retained an unquestionable superiority over their Arab counterparts, however modern their aircraft and advanced training in Russia.

In December 1969 the Israelis executed another spectacular 'James Bond' style operation. Reconnaissance units had located a newly erected Egyptian radar station on the western shores of the Gulf of Suez. From aerial photos the experts identified the installation as a new Russian type. Because of its threat to future air operations, it was essential to determine its technical characteristics. This was a classical mission for the paratroopers and a raid was mounted to 'lift' the complete station.

Landing silently by boat at night on the western shore of the Gulf of Suez, the raiding party overcome the guards and dismantled the radar station. Helicopters then arrived in the dark and hovering over the base they lifted off the entire secret tracking station and, while the troopers fought off Egyptian reinforcements, flew it back over the Gulf to the Israeli side. This operation was a severe blow to Russian electronic techniques and hardware.

Meanwhile the war along the banks of the Canal was reaching a new peak. More missile bases had been built and Israeli losses mounted daily. No sooner would the IAF destroy a site than the Egyptians, with Russian help, would replace it. The casualties weighed heavily on the morale of the Israeli population. Something had to be done to force the Egyptians to agree to a cease-fire. After considerable deliberation, it was decided to bring the war home to the Egyptian people, as they were being fed false propaganda through the government-controlled mass media, which claimed Egyptian victories limiting Israeli capabilities to fight.

At this time the coveted Phantom F-4 fighter-bombers began arriving from the USA. With this outstanding aircraft the IAF had at last received a versatile aircraft which was both an excellent interceptor and ground attack plane capable of carrying a heavy combat load. Besides carrying a large assortment of weaponry, the Phantom was also equipped with ultramodern electronic equipment for target acquisition and interdiction. These planes greatly increased the Israeli ability to strike at the heart of Egypt and bring the fighting to an end.

The first deep penetration bombing raids began in early January 1970. While Skyhawks pounded the canal-side artillery and fortifications, Phantoms streaked far into Egypt proper, attacking enemy camps and military installations in the Nile Valley, close to Cairo. A few days later, a massive attack on targets in the Cairo area inflicted great damage to stores of newly arrived equipment and munitions. The Egyptian Air Force reacted slowly and ineffectively while the Israeli Phantoms ranged unhampered through the Egyptian sky. The consternation in Egypt grew as the attacks progressed. On 13 January the Israelis attacked SAM sites just off Cairo International Airport while dozens of foreign correspondents looked on.

ATTACK PLANES OF THE 70s

Sukkoi SU-7BM (Egyptian markings). Seen here with a UV-16-57
55mm anti-tank rocket pod and external fuel tanks. It is also equipped
with 2 x 33mm internal cannons. This plane suffers from the common
fault of most Russian-built fighters — the lack of extended combat
range.

Skyhawk A-4H (IAF post-Six Day War camouflage). The IAF received
first the A-4E model in 1968 and later the above model, the A-4H,
which is believed to conform to many IAF specifications. This model
has improved avionics and a more powerful engine.

Mig-17F (1973 Egyptian markings). First received by the Egyptian
and Syrian air forces in the mid-fifties, it has proved a remarkably
durable plane. It was first utilized as an interceptor and has in
been modified to a ground-attack aircraft. It is still serving in the
Arab air forces.

Super Mystere B-2. This plane was the IAF's answer to the Mig-19
which the Arabs began to receive in the late fifties. Equipped with
2 x 30mm cannons and air-to-air missiles it served as an interceptor,
bringing down a number of Mig-17s, 19s and 21s. After the Six Day
War, the IAF had the Super Mysteres reengined with those of the
Skyhawk and extended its life as a ground-attack plane until after
the Yom Kippur War.

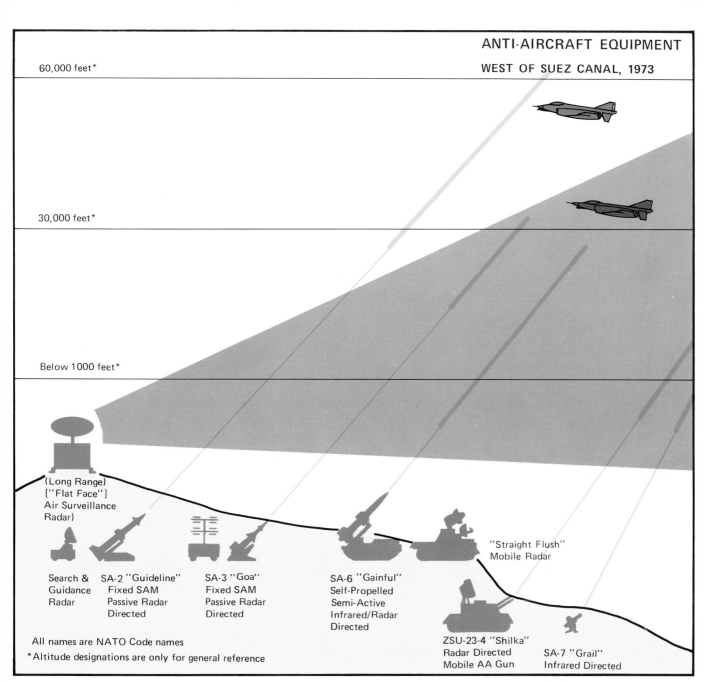

60,000 feet*

30,000 feet*

Below 1000 feet*

(Long Range)
["Flat Face"]
Air Surveillance
Radar)

Search &
Guidance
Radar

SA-2 "Guideline"
Fixed SAM
Passive Radar
Directed

SA-3 "Goa"
Fixed SAM
Passive Radar
Directed

SA-6 "Gainful"
Self-Propelled
Semi-Active
Infrared/Radar
Directed

"Straight Flush"
Mobile Radar

ZSU-23-4 "Shilka"
Radar Directed
Mobile AA Gun

SA-7 "Grail"
Infrared Directed

All names are NATO Code names

*Altitude designations are only for general reference

A SAM-2 being fired from a site in Egypt.

An Egyptian SAM-2.

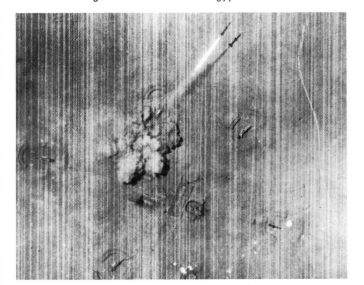

AGAINST THE ★RED PILOTS

When, in response to the IAF strategic deep penetration offensive, Soviet-manned Mig-21 air defense patrols made their appearance in the Nile Valley in the spring of 1970, the two sides arrived at an unofficial understanding which gave the Israelis a free hand extending to 20 miles west of the Canal. This unwritten agreement lasted until 25 July when two Russian-flown Migs jumped an IAF Skyhawk which immediately broke off its attack and evaded the interceptors. The identity of the pilots was determined by intelligence monitoring of their radio contacts. Following this encounter, a duel was inevitable between the Russian and Israeli pilots — each wanting to test the other.

On 30 July a flight of ground attacking Israeli Phantoms was intercepted by 16 Russian-piloted Migs. As the Phantoms broke to take on the Russians, Israeli Mirage fighters flying cover pounced on the overconfident Russians, and a swirling dogfight ensued.

According to one of the Israeli flyers, the Russians flew 'by the book', making themselves easy game for the experienced Israeli pilots. He recounts: 'They came at us in pairs and we let them pass in order not to be sandwiched between the pairs, as they had anticipated we would. They passed one after another as couples in a procession. We waited and got in behind, now sandwiching them, and had before us 16 Migs!

In this Mirage, IAF pilots have brought down eleven enemy fighters — ten Egyptian and one Syrian.

The sky was filled with planes as the formations broke up and the danger of collision was very acute. Also flying about were a lot of jettisoned fuel tanks, so you could hit anything if on our side. Then I saw by Number One fire a Shafrir missile and then another. Soon his target was on fire, spinning down from 30,000 feet, and the pilot bailed out fast.

'The melee continued, planes turning and twisting around, and firing guns and rockets at each other. More Israeli planes joined the battle. Braking hard, I succeeded in getting my sights on a Mig. He had guts and turned into the fight, but I quickly realized he was inexperienced. He made elementary mistakes. Diving down to 2000 meters, I cut him off and soon locked on my radar — then we had time. It was clear that he could not get away. At a range of 1000 meters we fired a missile. The Mig exploded into a flaming ball but, surprisingly, flew on. We fired another missile but this was no longer necessary. The Russian plane suddenly disintegrated in the air. The pilot ejected and I observed him swing down in his parachute. Breaking off combat I returned to base.'

Five Russian planes were shot down in a battle that lasted only a few minutes. There were no Israeli losses.

Finally the EAF made a show of force, but to little avail, and a number of Egyptian planes were shot down over the Delta with no Israeli losses. It was now the Egyptians turn to be frustrated but, as in all previous cases, the Soviets quickly bailed them out. The Russians realized the Egyptian helplessness and took over complete control of their air defense. Flying in men and equipment, the Russians built a massive air defense system integrating the most modern radar, high and low-level missiles, antiaircraft cannons, machine-guns and the latest model Mig-21J interceptors flown by Russian pilots. The system was built and manned by over 20,000 Russian servicemen stationed in Egypt for this purpose. The Israelis, in order to avoid confrontation with the Soviet Union, stopped their deep penetration raids into Egypt but, nevertheless, attacked and sank an Egyptian destroyer off Ras Bans in the Red Sea — a return flight of more than 1300 miles.

The Soviets did not limit themselves for long to guarding the skies of the Nile Valley against the IAF. They intervened directly in the fighting by moving their missile belt towards the Canal. Working 24 hours a day, they systematically built line after line of missile sites until they finally reached the Canal Zone. This encouraged the Egyptians to step up the fighting and late in June 1970 heavy fighting once more erupted, causing substantial casualties to the Israeli troops on the Bar-Lev Line. In response the IAF mounted a massive attack on the Egyptian positions. The Egyptians in turn, with high cover flown by Soviet fighter pilots, attempted low-level attacks on Israeli positions, but the IAF was ready for this move. IAF interceptors shot down two of the Egyptian fighter-bombers from under the high-flying Russians who did not venture to join the fighting.

During the first days of June 1970 a concentrated attack was mounted by the Israelis to cut off the northern Canal city of Port Said from the interior by aerially interdicting all bridges, roads and water pipelines leading to the city. The success of this offensive triggered off a clash between the Soviet Air Defense Command and the Israelis. The Russian missile sites now fired huge slavos of missiles at the Israeli planes as they flew into the attack, inflicting heavy losses of precious Phantoms and veteran crews. Though slowly pushed back towards the Canal, the IAF fighter-bombers continued to drop unprecedented quantities of bombs on the ground forces attacking the Israeli strongholds along the Canal.

After more than three years of inconclusive warfare, fighting between Israel and Egypt ended with a new American-sponsored cease-fire on 7 August 1970.

A McDonnell Douglas A-4E Skyhawk flying over the Dead Sea, the desert mountains of Jordan are in the background. These early model Skyhawks were armed with two 20mm Mk-12 American-built cannons and could carry about 3.5 tons of stores including various types of bombs, rockets, electronic warfare pods, smart bombs and external fuel tanks for extended flight time. First received by the IAF in 1968, these planes were used intensively against PLO terrorist bases and Jordanian army positions during the 1968/69 guerrilla war along the eastern frontier. Compare the A-4E with the later model A-4N on page 59.

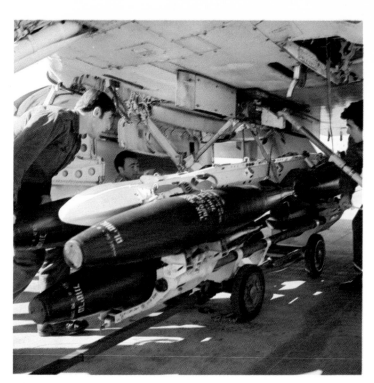

Right: *Cluster of 500-lb bombs on the centerline bomb rack of a Skyhawk. Red tapes will be pulled away when the bombs are finally attached to arm the bomb release mechanism.*

Below: *This Skyhawk is returning from a combat mission still carrying external fuel tank. Note the release wiring hanging from the outer right ordnance pylon, and cross type braking parachute. Just behind the main chute can be seen the drag chute which pops out first, catches the wind, and drags out the main braking chute.*

THE YOM KIPPUR WAR

Within 10 hours after the cease-fire became effective the Egyptians advanced their missile bases right up to the Suez Canal — in defiance of the military stand-still agreement. The lack of a forceful Israeli or American reaction seemed to confirm the widespread view that the cease-fire indicated an Israeli defeat.

The War of Attrition was the first Arab-Israeli conflict that did not end with a crushing defeat for the Arabs. This had great influence on Arab military strategy — bringing to an end the long period of deterrence by Israel's military superiority and encouraged the attack on Yom Kippur 1973.

Deeply influenced by Russian defense concepts, the Arabs regarded this missile array a counter to Israeli air supremacy. Now possessing hundreds of the latest Soviet SAM launchers, the Egyptians constructed an inter-locking air defense system that was the thickest and most effective, ever deployed — superior even to that protecting Hanoi during the American bombing offensive.

The older "Guideline" SAM-2 with its 20 mile range against high-flying aircraft was supplemented with the faster, more agile "Goa" SAM-3 batteries with a 17-mile range, to combat low-flying aircraft, by scores of the ultramodern, and mobile "Gainful" SAM-6 missiles mounted on armored carriers. The

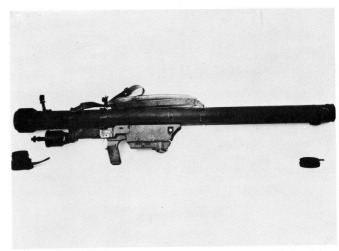

This Soviet-built SAM-7, NATO code-named 'Grail' shoulder launched antiaircraft missile was first seen in the Middle East during the War of Attrition 1969/70. The light weight (20 lb) A/A weapon with a range of about 2.5 miles and a speed of 1.5 mach. is designed for defense against low-level attacks.

SAM-6 is capable of rapidly changing position and radar frequency, thus making its location and destruction extremely difficult. An abundance of "Grail" SAM-7 shoulder-fired light AA missiles, also mounted in 8-barrel launchers on an armored chassis, together with the thousands of antiaircraft machine guns and radar-controlled multi-barreled cannons, completed the network. This complex formed an almost impenetrable air defense system.

Egyptian SAM-3s captured by Israeli forces on the west bank of the Suez Canal, October 1973. More modern than the SAM-2, the SAM-3, NATO code-named 'Goa', is effective from low to medium altitudes — 350 to 15,000 feet — supplementing the higher-flying SAM-2s. These missiles were integrated with radar directed antiaircraft cannons and machine guns, creating a tight antiaircraft network.

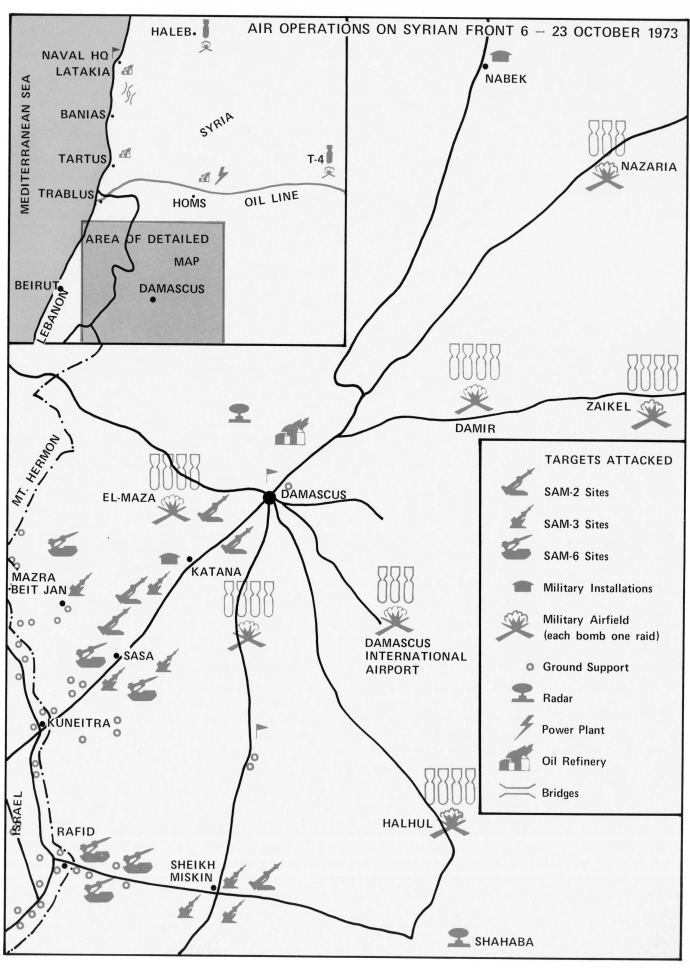

AIR OPERATIONS ON SYRIAN FRONT 6 – 23 OCTOBER 1973

MEDITERRANEAN SEA

HALEB.

NAVAL HQ
LATAKIA

BANIAS

SYRIA

NABEK

NAZARIA

TARTUS

T-4

TRABLUS

HOMS   OIL LINE

AREA OF DETAILED

MAP

DAMASCUS

BEIRUT

LEBANON

ZAIKEL

DAMIR

MT. HERMON

TARGETS ATTACKED

EL-MAZA

DAMASCUS

SAM-2 Sites

SAM-3 Sites

KATANA

SAM-6 Sites

MAZRA
BEIT JAN

Military Installations

DAMASCUS
INTERNATIONAL
AIRPORT

Military Airfield
(each bomb one raid)

SASA

Ground Support

Radar

KUNEITRA

Power Plant

Oil Refinery

ISRAEL

Bridges

RAFID

HALHUL

SHEIKH
MISKIN

SHAHABA

60

Above: *Bomb attack on Nazaria airbase in the north of Syria during the Yom Kippur War.*

Above Left: *Egyptian Mig-21 exploding from a hit by Israeli cannon fire. IAF fighter pilots preferred sharpshooting with their 30mm cannons over using their expensive and less personally satisfying air-to-air missiles.*

Left: *Syrian antiaircraft missile site some 25 miles southeast of Damascus, under heavy bomb attack. Note the many emplacements and trenches to guard it against attack from the ground.*

McDonnel Douglas F-4E ready for take-off.

The Commander of the IAF at that time was General Benny Peled, a highly experienced fighter pilot who had been shot down and rescued near Sharm el-Sheikh in the Sinai campaign of 1956. During the Yom Kippur War, his son, flying a Phantom, was also shot down and rescued.

The Arab air offensive began with Egyptian attacks on major installations in Sinai. Many of the attacks cost the EAF dearly. For example, on a fighter-bomber sweep by 12 Migs against Sharm el-Sheikh, patrolling Israeli fighters shot seven of the attacking Egyptian planes. At the same time, scores of Syrian fighter-bombers swooped in low over Israeli positions on the Golan Heights, attacking troops, vehicles and military camps.

The Arab air strategy was to prevent the IAF from concentrating its efforts. This was achieved by forcing it to spread its forces widely between distant battle fronts in order to support the scores of surrounded Israeli positions both in Sinai and on the Golan Heights. The Air Force was also called on to destroy or beat back the columns of invading armor and to retain air superiority over the battlefield. A desperate battle ensued in which the IAF had to fly thousands of sorties through the thick of the Arab air defense system.

Some 150 SAM-2 and SAM-3 missile batteries had

An A-4N Skyhawk II returning from a strike mission. The 'H' model is believed to incorporate many Israeli design specifications. When compared with the A-4E on page 51 it is easy to pick out the hump behind the cockpit which contains advanced avionics. Another difference is the shorter refuelling pipe extending from the nose. The latest A-4N (Skyhawk II) is much improved over the A-4H by installation of a more powerful engine giving it faster speed, shorter take off run, greater climbing rate and a heavier stores load. This engine is equipped with a smoke dissolving device which eliminates the smoke tracks which made the older Skyhawk easily sighted before an attack. Israeli Skyhawks are now armed with the Israeli-built DEFA 30mm cannons in place of the original 20mm ones. They also carry two Shafrir air-to-air missiles. During the early days of the Yom Kippur War these very sturdy subsonic planes made up the backbone of the IAF anti-missile strike force and sustained heavy losses in the intensive close-in attacks.

been set up in Egypt — more than 60 right along the Canal. Quite effective when fired in salvos at targets at higher altitudes, they forced the Israeli planes to come in low where they encountered a seemingly solid wall of antiaircraft fire from thousands of guns, SAM-7 shoulder-fired missiles and volleys of Sam-6s. All IAF plans to deal effectively with this anti-air umbrella were coming to naught, as most of the sorties flown were of ground support character. Realizing the grave situation of the country, the Israeli pilots, repeatedly flew into the heavy fire. Losses in the first days were so heavy that seeing the planes subjected to the shattering barrage of Arab missiles, the ground forces refused to call for more air support.

1. *Gun camera photo of Mig-21 hit by IAF interceptor. Israeli pilots preferred to sharpshoot with their 30mm cannons instead of using air-to-air missiles — especially in large scale melees with many planes dodging in and out.*

2. *An Egyptian Mig-17 on a ground-attack mission. This aircraft is loaded with two bombs and four air-to-ground missiles.*

3. *Mig-21PF in a tight turn. Using afterburners, he is either trying to break away to escape or to turn inside his pursuer and get on his tail.*

4. *An IAF Phantom closing in on an EAF Mig-17 over the Sinai. A rare photo taken by the Phantom's wingman.*

5. *A Mig-21 on IAF Mirage. Both aircraft are armed with air-to-air missiles.*

6. *An EAF Mig-17 returning from a ground-attack mission. Egyptian fighter-bombers were relatively ineffective because they just dashed in, tossed their bombs and fled before the omnipresent IAF interceptors could catch them.*

7. *An Israel Aircraft Industries — modified Mirage with the afterburners of its J-79 engine blasting. Armed with two Shafrir air-to-air missiles, this Mirage has dropped his external fuel tanks for better maneuverability.*

6.

7.

A most ferocious battle developed on the Syrian front, where the missiles were all concentrated along the border. Each attacking Israeli plane was subjected to salvos of dozens of SAMs. More planes were lost over Syria — 30 in one day — than in any combat zone thus far, but the pilots continued to attack the advancing Syrian armor columns.

As the IDF's holding action eventually stabilized the front, the hard pressed IAF could now reorganize and and systematically attack the missile sites. Damaged planes, many of them crash-landing on their return, were repaired as quickly as possible and sent back into action.

On the Egyptian front, the IAF pilots attacked the Canal bridges. But no sooner had they damaged a bridge, than the Egyptian engineers repaired it. It was an endless battle and losses were very heavy.

During the fierce battles of the first few days, the IAF lost half of the planes that were brought down during the entire war — all from ground antiaircraft. guns and missiles.

The losses were mounting on the other side as well. On 8 October alone, 29 enemy aircraft were shot down. In contrast to the Six Day War when most of the enemy planes were destroyed on the ground and

Israeli-modified Mirage in low-level maneuver to avoid Egyptian antiaircraft fire. This plane provided fighter cover for Israeli Skyhawks attacking missile sites along the Suez Canal in the Yom Kippur War. Note the two Shafrir AA missiles, external centerline fuel tank and one of two 30mm guns (seen as black spot just under air scoop). The black-bordered yellow triangles are identification markings to differentiate from Arab Mirages.* As the IAF received the American Skyhawk ground-support aircraft in 1968 and the very versatile Phantom fighter-bomber in 1970, the Mirage was employed primarily as an interceptor and cover aircraft for the at-tacking bombers. In the hands of the IAF pilots the Mirage proved to be superior to all fighter aircraft flown by the Arab air forces — including victories over Mig-21s flown by Russian pilots and Mirage IIIs and Vs with Arab, Pakistani, North Korean and Cuban pilots.

*According to foreign sources.

the pilots left unhurt, now the majority were shot down in combat and the pilots killed. The Arabs did not relish air combat and most air battles took place when enemy planes flying ground attacks were caught by Israeli interceptors. By the end of the war, of a total 222 Syrian planes downed, 162 were shot down in air combat; while the Egyptians lost 172 air-craft in the air, against 5 IAF planes. In comparison, during the Six Day War only 50 Arab planes were shot down in aerial combat for the loss of 10 IAF aircraft.

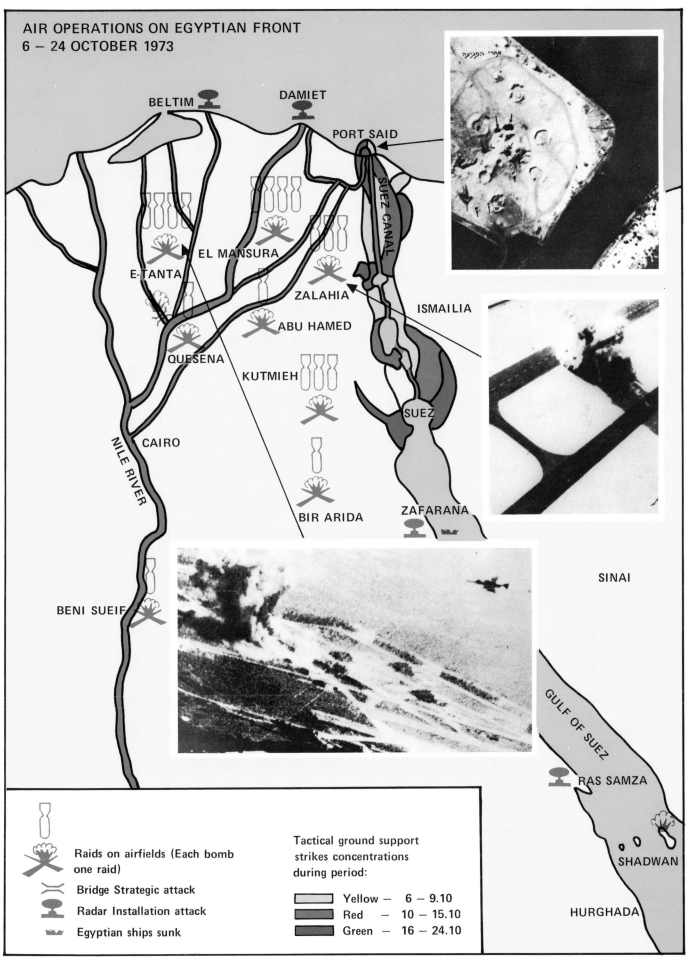

AIR OPERATIONS ON EGYPTIAN FRONT
6 – 24 OCTOBER 1973

BELTIM

DAMIET

PORT SAID

SUEZ CANAL

EL MANSURA

E-TANTA

ZALAHIA

ISMAILIA

ABU HAMED

QUESENA

KUTMIEH

NILE RIVER

CAIRO

SUEZ

BIR ARIDA

ZAFARANA

BENI SUEIF

SINAI

GULF OF SUEZ

RAS SAMZA

SHADWAN

HURGHADA

Raids on airfields (Each bomb one raid)

Bridge Strategic attack

Radar Installation attack

Egyptian ships sunk

Tactical ground support
strikes concentrations
during period:

Yellow — 6 – 9.10
Red — 10 – 15.10
Green — 16 – 24.10

Electronic and electronic countermeasure (ECM) weapons became an important element of the war between the IAF and the Arab air defense systems, reaching its highest level during the Yom Kippur War.

Above left & above: *SAM-6 'Gainful' transporter/launcher vehicle and Egyptian SAM-6 'Straight Flush' fire control radar.*

Above right: *An unusual photo of a surface-to-air missile exploding near an IAF Super Mystere during the Yom Kippur War. Though not actually hit by the missile, the plane was disabled by fragments and crashed.*

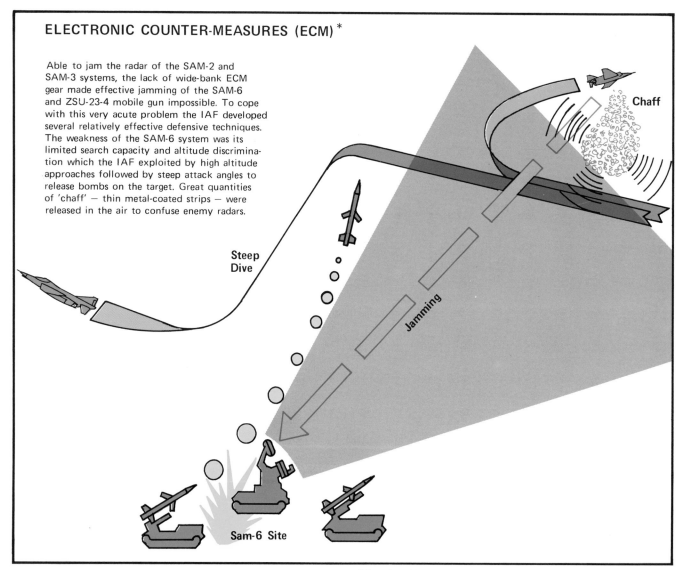

ELECTRONIC COUNTER-MEASURES (ECM) *

Able to jam the radar of the SAM-2 and SAM-3 systems, the lack of wide-bank ECM gear made effective jamming of the SAM-6 and ZSU-23-4 mobile gun impossible. To cope with this very acute problem the IAF developed several relatively effective defensive techniques. The weakness of the SAM-6 system was its limited search capacity and altitude discrimination which the IAF exploited by high altitude approaches followed by steep attack angles to release bombs on the target. Great quantities of 'chaff' — thin metal-coated strips — were released in the air to confuse enemy radars.

Chaff

Steep Dive

Jamming

Sam-6 Site

* Based on Foreign Sources only
(Air Warfare Book, etc).

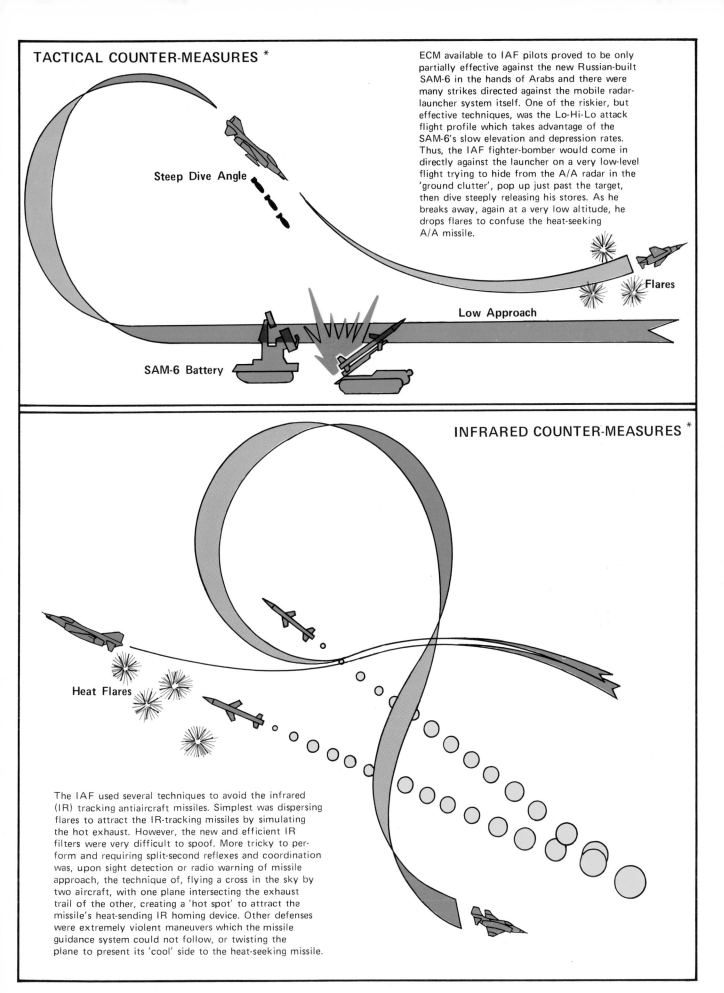

TACTICAL COUNTER-MEASURES *

ECM available to IAF pilots proved to be only partially effective against the new Russian-built SAM-6 in the hands of Arabs and there were many strikes directed against the mobile radar-launcher system itself. One of the riskier, but effective techniques, was the Lo-Hi-Lo attack flight profile which takes advantage of the SAM-6's slow elevation and depression rates. Thus, the IAF fighter-bomber would come in directly against the launcher on a very low-level flight trying to hide from the A/A radar in the 'ground clutter', pop up just past the target, then dive steeply releasing his stores. As he breaks away, again at a very low altitude, he drops flares to confuse the heat-seeking A/A missile.

Steep Dive Angle

Flares

Low Approach

SAM-6 Battery

INFRARED COUNTER-MEASURES *

Heat Flares

The IAF used several techniques to avoid the infrared (IR) tracking antiaircraft missiles. Simplest was dispersing flares to attract the IR-tracking missiles by simulating the hot exhaust. However, the new and efficient IR filters were very difficult to spoof. More tricky to perform and requiring split-second reflexes and coordination was, upon sight detection or radio warning of missile approach, the technique of, flying a cross in the sky by two aircraft, with one plane intersecting the exhaust trail of the other, creating a 'hot spot' to attract the missile's heat-sending IR homing device. Other defenses were extremely violent maneuvers which the missile guidance system could not follow, or twisting the plane to present its 'cool' side to the heat-seeking missile.

As part of the Arab offensive, scores of giant Russian-built helicopters filled with commando troops tried to seize strategic positions behind the Israeli front lines. Many of these helicopters were destroyed by defending Israeli aircraft. In all, some 40 helicopters were downed — these audacious efforts by the Egyptians produced little effort on the course of battle.

Another IAF feat was the shooting down of an air-launched Kelt missile fired at Tel Aviv from long range by an Egyptian Tupolev heavy bomber. The missile was observed in flight by two patrolling Mirage pilots, who shot it down into the sea.

A Syrian air attack on the northern settlements near Safed was foiled by interceptors who shot down three of the attacking Sukhoi-20 fighter-bombers. This was the first time that this type of plane had been seen in combat.

The Israeli Air Force now turned to the offensive. It set about attacking targets of strategic importance, mainly in Syria — systematically destroying oil installations, electric power stations and military camps throughout the country. In a retaliatory attack following Syrian bombardment of Israeli towns in the Jezreel Valley with "Frog" surface-to-surface missiles heavy damage was caused in Damascus. No more Frogs were launched.

בפגיעה

The Latakia oil terminals on the Syrian Mediterranean coast under heavy air attack. Retaliating with intensive air strikes after the Syrian surface-to-surface Frog missile attacks on Jewish towns in northern Israel, the IAF struck a heavy blow at the Syrian economic infrastructure during the Yom Kippur War.

Brake chute trailing, this Phantom returns to base.

Phantom F-4E (shark teeth are used by several squadrons). The Phantom is considered the heavyweight fighter-bomber of the IAF. This remarkable aircraft, holder of many world records, is both an excellent interceptor and capable of carrying external ordinance of more than seven tons. Equipped with the six-barreled M61A Vulcan 20mm gun, it also carries a variety of AAMs, bombs and electronic warfare instruments.

In the Sinai the IAF flew many sorties in ground support, first cleaning out the Egyptian sites in the northern sector and working southward. In all, some 40 out of a total of 60 sites were destroyed, most of them by air attacks. As the armor advanced into Egypt after crossing the Canal, the IAF was again operating freely over the battlefield. The enemy missile system which had taken so great a toll of the IAF was now broken and ineffective. Israeli control of the air was once more firmly established.

In the battles which raged through the Middle East's skies, the IAF flew four times as many sorties as in the Six Day War. Shooting down or destroying over 500 planes and losing over a hundred of its own. A clear and decisive victory was gained against the massive Soviet air defense system which defended the Arab battlefields. By the end of the war, the Israel Air Force had again won supremacy in the air against the heavy odds.

Above: Mig-21MF (Egyptian markings). This first line fighter was introduced into the Middle East in the early sixties. A mach 2+ interceptor, the Mig-21 is armed with two infrared homing Atol K-13 (AA2) air-to-air missiles and two improved radar directed Atols. It is the primary fighter craft of the Egyptian, Syrian, Iraqi and Lybian air forces.

Below: Mirage IIICJ (IAF camouflage colors used after 1968). The Mirage IIICJ was purchased from the French by the Israelis in response to the challenge presented by the Arab receipt of the Mig-21. It is equipped with 2 x 30mm guns and either one Matra R-530 or two Shafrir AAMs (seen in profile above) and a small variety of external stores. It is with this type aircraft that the IAF has maintained total air superiority over the Arab air forces since the Six Day War.

HELICOPTERS AT WAR

Helicopter warfare tactics developed in the Vietnam spurred the production of many new, more powerful and agile craft such as the heavy transport CH-53D, the Huey Cobra ground-attack and anti-tank helicopter, and the Russian Mi-24 Hind attack helicopter.

In the Middle East, the first heliborne attack was made by the Israelis on the artillery strongpoint of Um Kataf in eastern Sinai during the 1967 campaign. During the War of Attrition the Israel Defense Forces developed new tactics to track and destroy the guerrilla bands which infiltrated across the border from Jordan into the desert wilderness of the Judean Hills, and the mountains of the West Bank. On the Egyptian front, commando troops struck far into the Nile Valley.

Both sides learned their lessons well from these operations and as part of their surprise offensive in the October 1973 war the Syrians and the Egyptians made wide use of heliborne commando operations. Employing mainly the Mi-8, Arab commandos captured vital junctions and strongpoints on the Golan Heights and in Sinai, interfering with the movement of Israeli reinforcements. Though of momentary utility, these bold Arab commando operations were very expensive in men and machines and had no significant effect on the outcome war.

A Russian-built general-purpose medium helicopter to which the Egyptians attached a napalm cannister and used as 'kamikaze' planes in desperate attempts to destroy the IDF bridges across the Suez Canal during the Yom Kippur War. The Mi-8 proved to be ineffective as bombers and excellent as targets for Israeli ground troops.

The Israelis also executed heliborne operations deep inside Syria, including repeated ambushes on the Iraqi convoys moving to the Golan front. The last significant attack of the war was the successful IDF heliborne operation to take the summit and strongpoints of Mount Hermon.

Bell 205 landing at evening near a forward headquarters of an armored unit in Sinai.

A Bell 206 Jet Ranger hovering near a M-113 APC of an armor tactical headquarters. These helicopters rendered invaluable assistance in army cooperation during the fighting. Moving quickly from one position to another commanders could control vast operations, personally directing troops at decisive moments in battle.

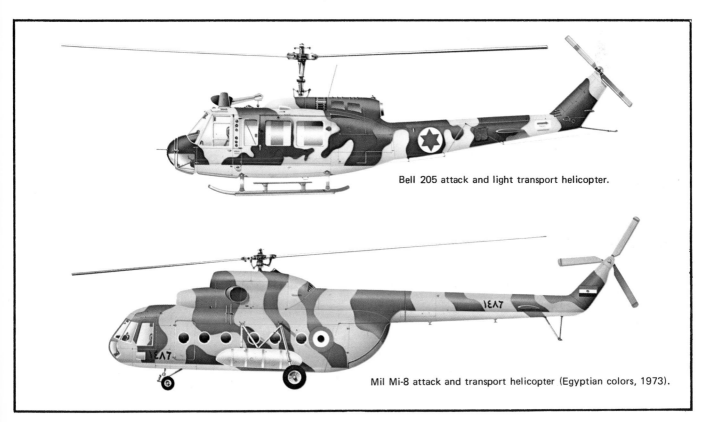

Bell 205 attack and light transport helicopter.

Mil Mi-8 attack and transport helicopter (Egyptian colors, 1973).

Above: *A Phantom on final approach before landing at base.*

Left: *A young Skyhawk fighter pilot descending from his cockpit, after combat mission. This is extremely intense duty and the pilots usually return soaking wet from their exertions. The ground is already 'turning around' the plane before the pilot hits the ground. In a few minutes this warplane will be ready for a new mission — with a fresh new pilot.*

Below: *Getting some well deserved shut-eye after combat flying. The pilot still wears his G suit and combat boots — ready for his next sortie.*

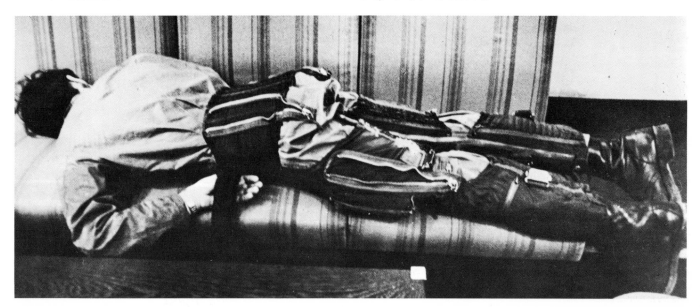

An Israeli-modified Boeing Stratocruiser refuelling A-4 Skyhawks. These transports were rebuilt by the Israeli Aircraft
Industries from the civilian version of the Boeing C-97 into
military transports, aerial tankers and surveillance
aircraft. On 17 September 1971 one of these electronic
surveillance Stratos was shot down by Egyptian SA-2
missiles 15 miles east of the Canal. In retaliation, the next
day the Israelis attacked seven missile sites along the Canal
with Shrike air-to-surface missiles. This was the only Israeli
attack against the Egyptian missile array between the War
of Attrition and the Yom Kippur War. The IAF Stratocruiser transports were modified so that the entire tail sec-
tion could be swung aside to permit loading out-sized cargos.
Unseen in this picture is a third refuelling terminal which
extends from the tail. Just forward from the tail can be
seen the observation bubble and window from which the
observer guides the fuel lines into the noses of the Skyhawks.

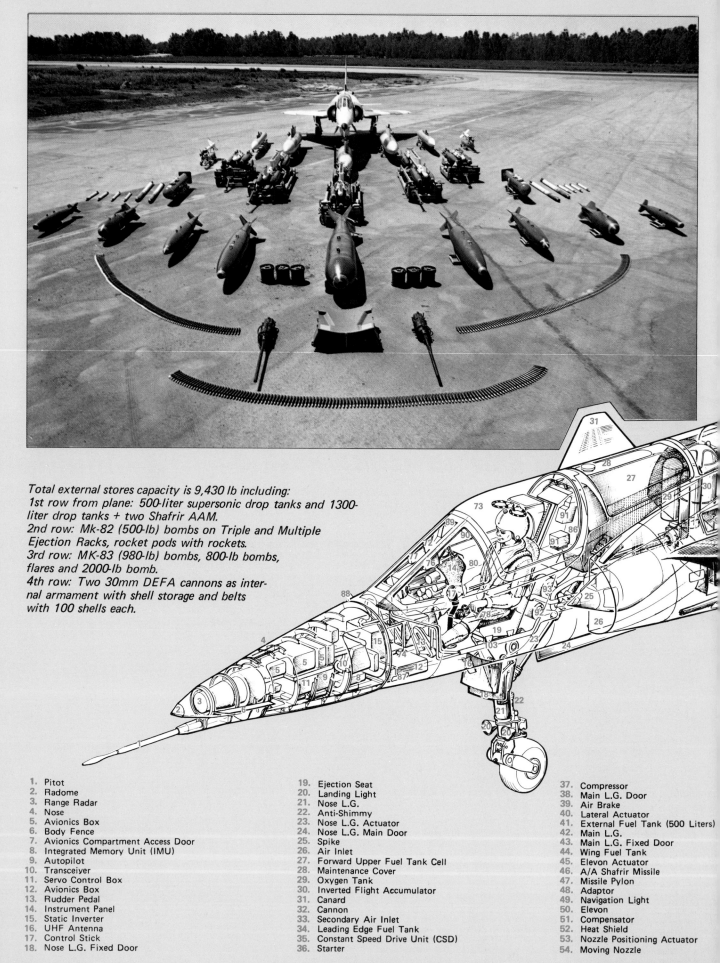

Total external stores capacity is 9,430 lb including:
1st row from plane: 500-liter supersonic drop tanks and 1300-liter drop tanks + two Shafrir AAM.
2nd row: Mk-82 (500-lb) bombs on Triple and Multiple Ejection Racks, rocket pods with rockets.
3rd row: MK-83 (980-lb) bombs, 800-lb bombs, flares and 2000-lb bomb.
4th row: Two 30mm DEFA cannons as internal armament with shell storage and belts with 100 shells each.

1. Pitot
2. Radome
3. Range Radar
4. Nose
5. Avionics Box
6. Body Fence
7. Avionics Compartment Access Door
8. Integrated Memory Unit (IMU)
9. Autopilot
10. Transceiver
11. Servo Control Box
12. Avionics Box
13. Rudder Pedal
14. Instrument Panel
15. Static Inverter
16. UHF Antenna
17. Control Stick
18. Nose L.G. Fixed Door

19. Ejection Seat
20. Landing Light
21. Nose L.G.
22. Anti-Shimmy
23. Nose L.G. Actuator
24. Nose L.G. Main Door
25. Spike
26. Air Inlet
27. Forward Upper Fuel Tank Cell
28. Maintenance Cover
29. Oxygen Tank
30. Inverted Flight Accumulator
31. Canard
32. Cannon
33. Secondary Air Inlet
34. Leading Edge Fuel Tank
35. Constant Speed Drive Unit (CSD)
36. Starter

37. Compressor
38. Main L.G. Door
39. Air Brake
40. Lateral Actuator
41. External Fuel Tank (500 Liters)
42. Main L.G.
43. Main L.G. Fixed Door
44. Wing Fuel Tank
45. Elevon Actuator
46. A/A Shafrir Missile
47. Missile Pylon
48. Adaptor
49. Navigation Light
50. Elevon
51. Compensator
52. Heat Shield
53. Nozzle Positioning Actuator
54. Moving Nozzle

KFIR C-2

A delta-winged mach 2.3+ single seat multi-mission combat aircraft incorporating canard surfaces, wing leading edge saw teeth and nose body fences. It has a stabilized combat loaded service ceiling of over 50,000 feet; a maximum take-off weight of 32,120 lb; combat weight with 50% internal fuel + two air-to-air missiles is 20,660 lb. The Kfir-C2 is powered by a single GE J-79 lightweight high thrust turbo-jet engine.

55. After Body	73. Canopy	91. Avionics Box
56. Drag Parachute	74. Angle-of-Attack Transmitter	92. ECS Turbine
57. Rudder	75. UHF Antenna	93. Water Separator
58. Rudder Actuator	76. Accelerometer Indicator	94. Transformer Rectifier
59. Vertical Stabilizer	77. Angle-of-Attack Indicator	95. AC Emergency Box
60. Anti-Collision Light	78. Throttle	96. DC Box
61. Leading Edge Saw Tooth	79. Hot Air Exhaust	97. Distribution Box
62. Engine	80. Cockpit	98. AC Circuit Breaker Box
63. Bleed Air	81. Fuselage Vertical Tail Fairing	99. Generator Control Unit (GCU)
64. Engine Compartment Cooling Scoop	82. Fuselage Wing Fairing	100. Hydraulic Tank
65. ECS Pre-Cooler Ram Air Scoop	83. Wing Front Beam	101. Front Upper Engine Connection Cover
66. Maintenance Panel/Door	84. Wing Main Beam	102. Wing-to-Fuselage Main Attachment Points
67. Wing	85. Ammunition Box	103. Cockpit ECS Pipe
68. Ingust Governing Vanes (IGV)	86. Cockpit Main Bulkhead	104. Avionics Box
69. After Belly Fuel Tank	87. Maintenance Access Door	105. Compensator-Actuator
70. Dorsal Fin	88. Pitot	106. Avionics Box
71. Fuselage Main Tanks	89. Emergency Compass	
72. Windshield	90. Clock	

Top & Bottom: *The world's hottest jet fighter — the McDonnell Douglas F-15A Eagle — in IAF colors. This newest addition to the Air Force was delivered in December 1976, each costing some 16 million dollars — without spare engines or parts, or any other ancilliary equipment. Their prime mission in the IAF is to guard Israeli airspace against intruding Arab or Soviet Mig-23s and Mig-25s. Pushed by two superpowerful GE J-100 jet engines, the Eagle has taken the world take-off and vertical ascent records away from its closest Soviet rival, the Mig-25 Foxbat. Its electronics are far more sophisticated than those of the Mig-25, including a 'head-up' display which projects radar blips and other computerized combat data directly onto the canopy so the pilot never has to take his eyes off the sky. Over the older Mig-23 the F-15 has an even more impressive edge. It outperforms the Mig-23 in speed (mach 2.5 to 2.3), maximum altitude (100,000 to 59,000 feet) and in every other important measure, including maneuverability.*

Above: *Pilot with rank of major in cockpit of F-15 completing pre-flight check. It appears that electronic instrumentation has practically replaced the pilot's eyes.*

Published by ESHEL-DRAMIT LTD.
P.O.B.115, Hod Hasharon, Israel
Telex: 32470 COIN-IL

Editorial Board: T. Eshel, S. Baskin, F. Rosenfeld
Production   : Israel Marketing
Layout   : Rita Geyer, A. Novitski
Photo Litho   : Shach-Offset Ltd.
Photo and Illustration Credits:
Israel Government Press Office; IDF Spokesman, Archives &
Photo Lab; 'Bamahane' (IDF publication); IAF Archives;
D. Rubinger; N. Gutman; M. Bar Am; E. Eyal;
'Soldat und technik' magazine and Israel Aircraft-
Industries Ltd.
Drawings by William Green of Pilot Press Ltd. London;
Sol Baskin, and Israel Aircraft Indusries Ltd.

Printed in Israel by Peli Printing Works Ltd.

ISBN-965-256-000-6